COMMIT TO THE LORD
WHATEVER YOU DO,
AND YOUR PLANS WILL SUCCEED
Proverbs 16:3

JENNY FISHER

JUST
Rewards

May God direct your life in the direction of your DREAMS

Just Rewards
Copyright © 2013
Pastor Jenny Fisher

Printed in the USA

Published By

GATEWAY PRESS

A Division of Aion Group Multimedia
and Gateway International Bible Institute

20118 N 67th Ave
Suite 300-446
Glendale AZ 85308
www.aionmultimedia.com

ISBN-10: 0985298650
ISBN-13: 978-0-9852986-5-4

To Contact Author
Pastor Jenny Fisher
P.O. Box 1993
El Mirage, Arizona 85335
(602) 290-3768
or e-mail the author at
jennyfisherministries@hotmail.com

or visit www.jennyfisher.org

TABLE OF CONTENTS

ACKNOWLEDGEMENT

Father God, above all else may you receive all the glory, honor, and praise. Your unfailing love has kept me from falling into the darkest abyss when confronted with emotional distress and physical abuse. Your light has sustained me and your words are my daily sustenance.

I wish to thank and acknowledge the following people who have been an immense blessing in my life and on this project:

With *special love* to my cherished son Daniel Santiago who has been my sidekick, my strength, and my inspiration. For without his encouragement this project would not have gone from my dreams to a reality. My son, my soul is delighted in you (Proverbs 29:17).

With *love* to my sisters Millie Baello and Nidia Nelson and their husbands, Juan Baello and David Nelson and children Sean, Christina & Michael, and Theresa & Jonathan and to my nieces, Angel and Mariana Wilson whose motivation and incredible insight proved to be invaluable.

With *special love*, for my dear departed mother and father, Juanita and Sixto Mendoza, whose love and strict upbringing made me the person I am today.

With *love and honor* to all the women, whom I have encountered and who have made an incredible impact in my life.

Finally, *thanks* to all those individuals who have made an impression in my life. To you I give special thanks and may God's blessing be upon you and your families always.

FOREWORD

Thank you for the honor to write your foreword Jenny. I pronounce a Father's blessing upon it and all who read it will feel the blessing of the Father's heart for them and His unconditional love. Your book is going to go far, I just know it! It is riveting and compelling! I couldn't put it down.. You have such an amazing life testimony Jenny! It needs to be shared with the whole world! You have been through so much pain and difficulty in such a short time, but NOW watch what God WILL DO... He is going to turn your lost and shattered dreams into a latter lifetime of fulfilled hopes and promises! He is going to meet your true hearts desires! He has such a wonderful and glorious plan for your life Jen. And in this latter day renewal of your life he has the 'right man' for the 'right time' for you. He will be a true king and priest of the Lord.

After reading your book more closely I can definitely see more clearly now what God has been showing me about you prophetically all this time. You are definitely called like Queen Esther of old but in this day and hour – "For such a time as this!" I am honored to be your Pastor, Spiritual covering, and your friend. May this book go farther and wider than you ever dreamed or expected it would go.

Love & Blessings!

Bishop Brian Alton
Pastors Brian & Phaedra Alton
Founding Senior Pastors / Bishop / Chancellor
Desert Rose Community Church
Gateway International Bible Institute

PREFACE

Dear Reader,

This book is dedicated to those who have, in any way been subjected to one form or another of physical or mental abuse. My heartfelt desire is for anyone reading the story and testimony of my life, to find comfort and ease in the inner most reaches of their hearts and minds by allowing each one to be touched by the powerful and everlasting goodness of our Lord Jesus Christ. I pray that the Lord and Savior Jesus Christ change your current situation to one that He desires for your life.

I hope it will help you understand God's plan for your life. God has given us universal laws to follow if we are to fulfill His desire in our life and receive the gifts of His promises. A life of daily thanksgiving, prayer, and praise to the divine Sovereign God, who's only desire is to bring salvation for any who have not known Him, and the promise of not only a free but abundant and eternal life in Christ Jesus.

Have faith to believe in God's wondrous and everlasting promise. Though times may be tough, and hard with sorrow, seek God's guidance in all your troubles. For if you believe, and stand firm in your faith, upon you will rain God's mercy, blessing and grace.

Warmly,

Jenny Fisher

Chapter One

INTRODUCTION

The Early Years

As a child growing up in the 1960's, my small world was stormy. My parents were Puerto Rican immigrants who arrived in New York in the 1940's chasing the American dream. Mom and Dad only had an elementary grade education, yet they were determined to ensure an easier life for their five children. My first recollection was at the age of three. I was sitting on the floor at the entryway to the kitchen in our small apartment playing with my toys while my oldest sister was cooking dinner on the stove.

I was born at Mount Sinai Hospital on the island of Manhattan, New York. I, along with my brother and sisters, lived in a small apartment. My father worked several jobs to provide for his family's welfare. My mother was a stay at home mom. She watched over and cared for us, as any stay at home mom would do. There were strict household rules which I and my siblings adhered to. Disciplinary action was not taken lightly. If anyone of us conducted ourselves less than regimented we knew the consequences. First we were scolded. If we continued to maintain an undisciplined attitude, we were then subjected to harsh (for lack of a better word) spankings. Those disciplinary actions, although severe, prepared me for a future of disappointment and abuse.

My parents were not very affectionate in the sense of the word, yet I recall, although rare, my mother stroking my hair when I placed my head on her lap. Dad was rarely home, or so we thought. He arrived late in the evenings after we were asleep and left early in the morning before we awoke. Dad was constantly working day and night without regard for his health; his main objective, to enhance the future of his family. So in 1968 we moved into a brownstone style home in Queens. We were moving on up! The houses' architecture was like all the other houses on the block, the only difference was the colors; ours was white with the lower portion of the house painted green. Long hair was in and miniskirts were worn short.

The fall of 1970 arrived swiftly. On one rare occasion my father invited me to travel with him into town. A small gesture which meant the world to me and produced in me a feeling of joy, as I looked forward towards spending quality time with him. My little heart began pounding as we boarded the train headed towards the business district. It was such a wonderful adventure; my mind soaring with great imagination during the ride downtown. When we finally arrived at our destination, a massive exodus occurred. My little hand clutched inside my fathers' as we headed towards the stairs, emerging into a sea of bright sunshine, surrounded by the flurrying of the hustle and bustle of city life. My mind awoke to new thrills, as my eyes scurried in all directions absorbing every detail of my surroundings. Walking towards what seemed like an eternity before finally reaching our objective - a used car lot.

Dad began searching the lot until his eyes became fixed on an old 1960 Ford truck. He walked around the truck absorbing every detail. I mirrored his every footstep. He stopped in front of the truck, his hand searching for the latch. Unlatching the hood he pushed the hood up in an open position; while one hand held the hood open his head moved forward, deeper into the mouth of the truck. Dad paid close attention to the engine and its internal hoses and components. Gently lowering the hood, he purposely ensured the hood was securely latched, before maneuvering towards the drivers' side door. His hand swung up and gripped the door handle. He pushed the button in and opened the door. Peering into the interior cab, he inspected the dashboard, all the while asking if I liked it. "Sure, dad," I said, not truly understanding what he was doing.

The exterior of the truck was dark maroon in color and the interior seat was finished in red. Dad paid a handsome price for the truck; a total of $3,000.00, which was considered a king's ransom at that time. Our family's transportation was either by bus or subway, so when I realized that Dad was in the process of obtaining a family vehicle, the awareness stimulated excitement within me. Dad headed into the dealership and proceeded to negotiate the deal. As I watched, I noticed the legal tender used was cash in completing the transaction. Dad had a big grin on his face when he picked me up and carried me over to the truck. "Is this ours now…Dad?" I asked. Putting me down he looked me in the eyes and replied "Yes, it is." He opened the door and I hopped into the passenger side of the truck. I searched Dad's face as he drove away from the used car lot that day, my little body bouncing up and down on the red bucket seat. What I found on Dad's face was the satisfaction in completing what he set out to do that day.

When we arrived home, I ran inside and called my sister to come out and look at what Dad bought. The air was filled with enjoyment and delight throughout the house. That night Mom and Dad sat us down after dinner and began to share with us their reasons why they bought the truck and why a decision was made to move us to Puerto Rico. Their decision was based on several factors. The move would allow us to experience whilst educating us in our heritage, culture, history, food and music. "Wow," I thought. This news was even more thrilling than Dad buying the truck!

Dad's first project was to embark on preparing the truck for the move. He constructed a large wooden crate within the bed of the truck. Mom and Dad then sold the house with most of our possessions. When the work on the truck was completed, everything remaining was packed into the truck. The truck was then locked up and secured and shipped by sea through Sea Train. On the day of our move, the family mounted into a taxi and headed towards JFK Airport. The first time I ever took a trip on a plane was the day we boarded the Pan Am flight headed to Puerto Rico. Growing up in New York had become a comfortable way of life with school friends and neighbors. Moving to Puerto Rico was to be an altogether different experience from the life I knew.

Learning a whole new language, culture and set of rules was quite overwhelming. My first semester in school was the sixth grade. Unable to speak a word of Spanish, it was extremely difficult to adjust. Nevertheless, the more I thought about it, the more I came to one conclusion; I had to succeed in my studies in order to advance into the next grade. Failing was not an option. Not wanting to repeat the same grade and deal with the same teachers, I rationalized and established my priorities. I set out to learn all that I could about my heritage and cultural enlightenment and for the next four years I absorbed all my country had to offer, its music, dance, art, customs, traditions and ethnicity.

Even though my youngest sister and I were trying to acclimate to the change both in school and at home, it seemed that arguing and fighting was part of our daily ritual. My father rented a house upon our arrival in a small town named Pajaro (Bird). The house was adjacent to the towns' baseball field. The property line was divided with a four foot chain link fence. The entrance to the baseball field was parallel midway to the back of our house, the home team bleachers just several feet away. Home games allowed for the area around the bleachers to be used for neighbors to congregate and enjoy all night socializing. Sitting on the back steps of the house provided a perfect view of the home games when the team was in town.

Since our house contained no internal plumbing, we had to immediately adjust to the fact that easy accessibility to both the shower and outhouse was not possible as both were located at the exterior of the house. The shower consisted of a small one room hut located fifteen feet from the rear steps to the main house. The fabrication and assembly of the shower hut was neither sturdy nor of durable construction. Inexpensive wood was used during construct. The distance between the wood slats were not appropriately spaced leaving gaps between them. The main door to the hut faced the home game bleachers. Showers were usually taken before the sun set. I felt so embarrassed every time I had to sneak out of the house to take a shower during a home game. Moving nonchalantly as possible hoping no one looked over their shoulders and noticed me.

"Hooray, I did it!" I would think, as I opened the door and crossed the threshold into the hut. Once inside I immediately hung the towel horizontally across the wood slats protecting me from any unwanted gawks. I turned on the water and "Aaahhh…the water was cold!" There was no hot water.

Can you imagine how I, as a little girl must have felt at the end of the shower? Having only one towel, I had to first wipe down the water off my body with my hands, much like a squeegee does. Next, I wrapped the towel around me and held it tightly with one hand, while carrying my clothes with the other hand; maneuvering much like a trapeze artist in hopes of successfully opening the hut door. When that feat was accomplished, I opened the door as quietly as possible and walked towards the rear stairs, whispering to myself reassuring words "You are doing great!" Trying to keep my eyes focused on arriving at my destination without tripping or losing my towel. This feat was an everyday occurrence.

The outhouse was located at the rear edge of the property as far back from the house as possible. Just beyond third base. Since the bathroom (shower and outhouse) was physically located on the exterior, no electrical consideration was given when constructed. The outhouse was built on a concrete slab which housed a plastic toilet located in one corner. The structural wood enclosure stood on six legs with a one foot gap around the bottom of the entire enclosure providing ventilation. The roof was made of a zinc metal. A gas lantern or flashlight was mandated when unexpected trips to the outhouse were necessitated after dark. Arms swung wildly in front of my face to protect me from the fierce flurry of mosquitoes looking for blood whenever the cover was first lifted exposing them to fresh air.

Late one afternoon I had just left the confines of the outhouse, when my sister walked past me in that direction. As she walked past I yelled "Next!" Laughing…I was halfway to the house when I heard my sister screaming. I ran back to see what had happened. When I entered the outhouse, my sister was hanging for dear life onto the interior side wall of the outhouse; her legs dangling over the excrement and waste matter within the pit of what was left of the interior of the outhouse. The concrete floor had collapsed! "Oh my God," I said. Mom…Dad, help me!" Grabbing onto her waist I pulled her to safety. Her leg scratched from the rebar as it rushed past it in a downward movement towards a horrifying and unthinkable death. Her quick catlike agility equipped her to cling somehow to the wall. Pulling her to safety and clutching onto each other we emerged from the outhouse as Mom and Dad reached us. Our screams heard by both our parents and our neighbors. Mom escorted us into the house while Dad stayed outside with the neighbors working on the outhouse. It was only through God's grace that my sister managed to survive a certain death. In looking back, I honestly believe both my sister and I were protected by God who watched over us that faithful day.

It was not long after the incident at the outhouse that my parents decided to move us to a newly built residential community which housed all the modern conveniences. The community was known as Levittown. Years went by and as the date for my ninth grade graduation became closer, my excitement grew. I was going to attend Bayamón High School. The excitement derived from the knowledge that I would finally be able to wear pants to school! Amazing, how small things turn out to be what matters the most.

Graduations are meant to be a joyful event, yet on that special day I did not consider it a happy one. I had recently broken up with a boy I was dating; I was so heartbroken. Octavio was the boys' name. His stature was tall. He was also dark and handsome. My reasoning was no longer rational. I was so distraught by the breakup; all I wanted to do was escape. The only recourse easily accessible to drown my heartache, were cigarettes. My habit started at the age of fifteen. Both my parents smoked making it an easy habit to attain. My first cigarette was a Marlboro red. I did not specifically like the Marlboros', so I tried other brands such as Chesterfields, Cools, and finally Tareyton 100's. No brand was better than the other, so I chose the Tareytons'. Cigarettes became my number one vice for well over 25 years.

It was shortly after my graduation that my parents called a family meeting. On this occasion it was to inform us of their intentions to relocate. "Where," I asked? "California…Santa Barbara to be exact," Dad said. There was no arguing with Mom or Dad when they reached a decision. I was shocked by their news. I neither anticipated it nor expected it. "No matter," I thought. Nothing seemed to be working for me anyway. The healing process associated with my breakup was slowly taking place. So mulling over the information of our future relocation shifted the restorative process gears and encouraged an increase of healing adrenalin. "Maybe it is for the best," I thought. The more I contemplated the idea, the more I welcomed the change. The period of time I lived in Puerto Rico with my family was an incredible experience. The food, culture, beaches, festivities, music, and its extraordinary people will always be entwined within the very fabric of my heart, mind and soul.

We boarded a plane headed towards the Los Angeles International Airport in December 1974. What an amazing experience to be back in a large city. Any lingering emotional despair because of my breakup disappeared upon exiting the plane and walking into the incredibly larger and busier airport terminal. After several weeks of lodging with relatives, the family settled down in Panorama City, a city just north of Los Angeles. It was magnificent to be back in a city with modern conveniences. One never knows what one possess' and takes for granted until circumstances change, all conveniences are eliminated leaving one with only the bare essentials.

Living in L.A. County was an incredible rush. It welcomed me with open arms. The night life was hopping. Partying was part of my nightly routine. Attending school full time and working full time, left me with four hours a night to carouse before heading home for a two hour nap; arising fully to commence once again, my customary ritual. I began experimenting with several different types of drugs. I enjoyed smoking pot, especially Tai. As a result, three years elapsed quickly and without, I am happy to say, incident. Whether or not I was dabbing into drugs, my studies were always a priority, and as a result I fulfilled my academic requirements a semester early. Completing my studies early only provided additional freedom to enjoy my pastime which was smoking marijuana.

Although, I was absent from school during the last semester, I returned in June 1977 to participate in the commencement ceremony graduating with a full scholarship. It was not until many years later that I was introduced to cocaine, speed, angel dust, sex and alcohol. At the end I preferred speed, which provided the energy to maintain the lifestyle I was comfortable with. Since no one is capable of predicting one's future, one only attempts to formulate the best possible decisions for one's life. Nevertheless, those decisions are the medium by which one's future is ordained.

Little did I know the roads I was destined to undertake…

My First Marriage - Wesley

I married young, although at the time I didn't think so. The date was October 31, 1977, four months after I graduated from high school. He was a young Marine named Wesley. I was a young starry eyed girl with big dreams marrying a tall handsome serviceman. We married in a small Chapel in Los Angeles with a small reception held afterwards. Only family and close friends attended. It was a quick wedding as we had only a short time before reporting to his next assignment. Waking early the next morning, our things packed, we headed east to meet his family, spending a week visiting the wonderful attractions New York City offered. I was sad to leave the appeal and alluring charm of the city as the week came to an end.

Heading towards a new future and a fresh start, we boarded a plane to Puerto Rico. Wesley's first assignment was located on a marine base on the small island of Vieques, just off the main island of Puerto Rico. Arriving at the main airport in San Juan, we chartered a two engine plane to fly us across to Vieques. Upon arriving at the air field we mounted a taxi and proceeded directly to the base. Since it was Wesley's first assignment, he was unaware of the procedures needed to obtain housing on base. Our hope shattered when confronted with the news of no base housing readily available. In spite of that, if we so desired they would place us on a waiting list. "What were we to do?" I thought. We were so unprepared for the news. Leaving the base we headed towards the town of Esperanza (Hope) in hopes of locating an apartment before the sun went down.

There were not many apartment complexes in town. The first complex we visited had no vacancies. The second complex contained one tiny apartment for rent. The number of units comprising this complex totaled six. The building rested directly on the beach. The ocean waves foaming into miniature bubbles as they rolled onto the coast line shore only several feet away. The bedroom windows had an incredible ocean view. The size of the apartment was no bigger than four hundred square feet and consisted of two rooms. These two rooms were then divided into halves. Crossing over the main door threshold placed you directly in the living room/kitchen area. This room was divided by a wooden laminated countertop on four legs. A small stove and refrigerator made up the remaining tiny kitchen.

Maneuvering through the living room took no more than three large steps to be within the adjacent small bedroom and bathroom. The room was only capable of sustaining a full size bed in one corner while the other corner housed a small opened faced wooden cabinet designed to accommodate clothing. The bathroom's décor was unfinished concrete. It was not much to look at, yet at that juncture, I was delighted to find a furnished apartment on our second attempt an hour before the sun descended.

The base was located on the other side of the island and provided all the amenities necessary for the men and women stationed there, including hot water. It was an entirely different matter for those living within the town limits. The town was supplied water to cook, clean, launder and bathe between the hours of ten o'clock in the morning and two o'clock in the afternoon only. The water supplied within that time period was neither hot nor filtered. Resources such as a water filtration system or fresh water pipeline used on the main Island were non-existent. It was for that reason the townspeople had no other choice than to use seawater piped in as part of their daily lives.

Only one coin laundry shop existed in the middle of town. Locating a taxi cab or bus within the town limits was impossible. Most of the taxis were stationed at the airport. This of course proved difficult when several loads of laundry needed washing. At first, it was an incredible impossibility to carry all the gathered laundry, supplies and hauling everything to the center of town in one trip. It did, however, eventually become easier once I developed a routine and asked Wesley to wash his uniforms on base. Childhood memories of living in Pajaro with my parents' years earlier flooded my senses.

Wesley would wake up every morning and head towards the base to start his day. I, on the other hand spent my day within the tiny confines of our apartment; only departing when laundry day arrived or heading towards the commissary located on the army base on the mainland. I was forbidden to fraternize with my neighbors or leave the apartment for any reason other than errands. I was becoming more and more claustrophobic with each passing day. When Wesley arrived home in the evenings he was tired. Since there were no theaters, shops or anything to occupy one's mind within the town limits, I occasionally asked Wesley to take me to see a movie on base. "No," he would respond. "I worked all day…I'm too tired."

Every so often, I asked Wesley to lend a hand around the apartment, but Wesley refused. As the days wore on, I became more irritable. Attempting to control my emotions after Wesley refused to assist me was a huge undertaking. Although Wesley had all the comforts on base, his selfishness prevented him from bringing fresh water from base when asked. I had no other choice than to boil water daily for drinking and bathing. His unwillingness to provide support led only to bickering, and constant arguments. I began to notice a change in him as his jealous and controlling nature began to surface. His physically abusive tendencies arouse whenever the situated dictated to conceal his infidelities.

It was several months into our marriage when Wesley approached me and told me I needed to be seen by a doctor. When I asked him "Why," he said "Because you have to." Going to the hospital was not an easy task. We had to find someone going in the direction of the ferry, or walk miles to get there. Although the island is separated from the southeast coast of Puerto Rico by eight miles of sea, the ferry ride from Fajardo totaled eighteen miles of sometimes stormy weather. When the ferry docked we disembarked and walked towards the Army hospital. It was several miles of scenic road so the walk was refreshing after the ride. As we moved closer to the hospital I noticed it was located at the top of a hill with an incredible view.

We checked in with the nurse and sat down to wait. I was still unsure of "Why" I was there and as those thoughts flowed through my mind, Wesley was called in to see the doctor. My name was called fifteen minutes later. The nurse led me to a room to wait for the doctor. "Finally," I thought "Now…maybe I'll find out what is going on." After a twenty minute wait, the doctor walked in. He was tall, semi balding with black rimmed glasses firmly fixed upon his aquiline nose. His hooded eyes were of a soft brown color. The normal formalities out of the way, he began to discuss the reason I was there. His speech was formal and monotone; as if what he was about to relay was a normal occurrence. "Okay," I said. "Why am I here?" He broke the shocking news by saying "This is just a precaution; you will be given a shot of penicillin along with antibiotics in pill form". "Why I asked" stunned. "Well," the doctor said. "Your husband contracted some form of venereal disease and has probably past it on to you. As a result, it is required that anyone who has been in contact with him receive antibiotics and a shot." I looked at him in disbelief. My first thought was "Why did he do this to me?" My body instantly turned numb as the needle penetrated my skin. My mind became oblivious to my surroundings as I grasped the reality of what the doctor had just relayed. Shaking me he said "Mam…mam are you okay?" Jerking myself back to reality, I said…"Yes…I'm okay."

The doctor left. I gathered my things while still in a state of disbelief. Walking out of the exam room I headed towards the waiting room. As I sat down, I felt the uncontrolled rage developing within the deepest recesses of my being. Anger growing in its intensity as the minutes passed; giving way to hundreds of unimaginable thoughts. Unable to calmly deal with the situation, I gave into the emotional fury of the moment. Pacing the waiting room, I wondered "Why doesn't he come out of there already!" "What is taking so long?!" "Why is Wesley still in with the doctor?"

I was deep within my rage when at last; the doctor appeared in the waiting room. He sat me down and slowly began to speak. He informed me that Wesley had a severe allergic reaction to the penicillin. His heart stopped. The doctor had no other choice than to give him another shot to counteract the first one while reviving him. "Great!" I said. "Why did that happen? I wanted to kill him myself!" The doctor said "Why don't you relax, get some coffee. It will be a while before your husband is free to go home."

Introduction

Heeding the doctor's advice, I walked around the hospital grounds trying to occupy my time. Having partially observed all there was of the hospital, I walked towards the waiting room to wait. Three hours had passed before Wesley emerged from the inner sanctions of the doctor's office. I looked up from where I was sitting. Wesley walked towards me; his shoulders drooped, his face ashen and drained of all color. His hair was disheveled, his clothes rumpled. If his expectation was one of "Oh...poor Wesley," he was sadly mistaken. His recent brush with death did little to change my position on his unfaithfulness and lack of respect for our wedding vows. At last the opportunity to execute my emotional discharge upon him was within my reach. In an instant my mouth opened and a flurry of unsavory innuendoes and metaphors gushed out at Wesley. Unable to quench the anger still raging within me, I stormed out of the hospital.

Shocked at my verbal explosion, Wesley followed me out and caught up with me. His self-absorption, arrogance and pride were injured when confronted with the truth of his infidelity. The argument grew into shouts of fierce hostility. Then before I knew it he lifted his hand and slapped me again and again...hard. There was no need for physical abuse. Wesley was six foot four inches tall and I was five feet four inches. "Stop," I yelled. "Are you going to shut up?" Wesley said. "Why did you do this to me? Who did you sleep with?" "I said...shut up!" Wesley shouted. "No," I shouted back and ran as fast as I could. He chased after me, yelling "WHY ARE YOU RUNNING...YOU HAVE NO PLACE TO GO!" his long strides closing the distance between us.

He was almost upon me as we neared the ferry. Worrying about what he would do to me, I was determined not to become another statistic. I don't know how, but at that instant I managed to obtain a burst of energy...a second wind. It was the burst of energy I needed to increase the distance between us and climb onto the waiting ferry. As I mounted the ferry, I turned and noticed Wesley calmly walking towards the boat; his face expressing an arrogant smirk. Physical assault became a simple and resourceful way to bring any argument to a close without further explanation. Wesley's desire of a good wife was a tacit, submissive and helpless woman. A woman fashioned through ill-treatment and manipulative means; quite the opposite of my strict independent upbringing.

Although Dad was considered a stringent disciplinarian, I wanted someone with a softer nature. My heartfelt yearning for such a man was not sufficient to materialize him. In fact, unbeknownst to me I was destined to go through life as a magnet enticing and luring violent and dishonest characters.

One morning I was in the kitchen making coffee when Wesley walked in. Since his movement was non-threatening I was caught by surprise when he grabbed my arm. Shocked…I looked at him. The eyes are the mirrors into one's soul and what I saw in Wesley's eyes revealed his disdainful and possessive character emerging. That morning insecurity sparked his controlling disposition and reiterated, through clenched teeth, forbade me to leave the apartment and kept me a prisoner. Walking across the hall to visit with the female neighbor or going for a stroll was out of the question. My daily movements were constantly monitored. Insecurity governed his personality and provoked apprehension and hostility within our marriage. Even though my social calendar was non-existent, it did not procure him from preserving his suspicious beliefs. Distrust is only a person's own unconscious insecurities developing into conscious form.

Our apartment was no longer a home, it became my prison. Yet, even in the midst of all the chaos something extraordinary happened. My internal clock was set in motion and my motherly instincts succeeded in taking precedence over my entire life. Consciously I was aware of the importance of conceiving a child from this relationship. Was it necessary for survival? I did not know. I didn't question it. The instinct was there and the instinct was a true blessing for it turned out to be my saving grace.

After many months of trying several different techniques I finally managed to become pregnant. The year was 1978. Saturday Night Fever was recently released and was playing in the theaters on the mainland.

Introduction

One evening I noticed Wesley getting dressed. I asked him if I could go with him. He turned around, looked me in the eyes and said in a clear flat voice "NO, you are staying home." "Where are you going?" I asked. "I am going to see the movie - Saturday Night Fever. I'll be home tomorrow." Wesley responded. "Why can't I go with you?" I replied. "What part of NO don't you understand?" He shouted angrily. Appalled at his response, I walked away. He had made plans to go to the mainland earlier in the day without me. He finished dressing and headed out the door, leaving me behind in our dreary tiny apartment.

Several weeks later after Wesley's movie escapade, my neighbor across the hall knocked on my door while Wesley was at work. Although I was surprised at her visit, I welcomed it. I put on a pot of coffee and sat down to enjoy our visit. The conversation started just like any other conversation would. We discussed the weather, family, friends, and then she gradually worked her way to ask me "So…when was the last time you went the movies?" My cup froze in mid-air. I looked at her and said "I haven't been to see a movie in a while…why?" "Well…I have to tell you something," she said and put forth the details of Wesley's infidelity. I knew my suspicions were being confirmed as her unrelenting story telling spewed out. "I'm sorry… however, I thought it best you knew," she said and took her leave. "Again," I thought as I closed the door behind her. Finally I had enough ammunition. No longer would I allow myself to be the recipient of any further physical or emotional abuse. I contacted my folks and asked if I could come home. Mom and Dad were excited and provided a one way ticket home to California. A week later, I mustered enough courage and waited until Wesley left for work before I packed all of my belongings. Leaving a note on the kitchen counter, I mounted a taxi headed towards the airport and freedom.

15

My Saving Grace - Daniel

Upon my return to California I moved in with my oldest sister. I was so thrilled to be pregnant! I didn't know why at the time, it just felt right. I can remember on three separate occasions in which I had specific dreams announcing that I was to expect a baby boy. The dreams were so vivid and incredible. In fact, what stood out in each of the dreams were two large sparkling blue eyes looking up at me through the illusion of water. I perceived the water as spiritual.

After my feelings of failure in my marriage, the dreams provided me with great comfort. I believe it was through those dreams, God reached out to me in his magnificent wisdom to bless me with a son. Since God knit me together in my mother's womb (Psalm 139:13), I was given exactly what I needed, at the exact time to preserve my life - my son.

Although I was never a debut Catholic during my young life, I always believed God watched over me while quietly directing me towards Him. One day I was having difficulties in choosing a name for the baby. Although Wesley and I had previously spoken about it, I disagreed with him and decided not to name the baby Wesley George. I instinctly knew the baby was to receive an altogether different name. Unsure of what the baby's name was to be, I turned the television on during Easter Sunday in 1978. Religious movies have always interested me and in the midst of one, a small voice became audible in my mind. The voice repeated the name of Daniel. The story of Daniel was being played out on the screen. Each time I tried to shake the voice away, it grew in intensity. "Ok, enough… already," I said. "I heard you." "Yes, I agree Daniel is a good name." Fine, the baby will be called "Daniel." Suddenly a great peace enveloped me the instant I decided to call the baby…Daniel.

Even though the date for Daniel to arrive during the Christmas season had past, I was not concerned. I knew he would arrive when he was ready. On December 31, 1978, my sister decided to throw a New Year's Eve party. As any Puerto Rican knows, call one person to spread the news of a party and you'll soon have a full house. The festivities were lively; people dancing to the salsa music streaming from the record player. It was almost midnight on New Year's Eve when my Dad asked me to dance. He said "Come on girl let's dance." "Isn't it about time that baby comes out?" I was not given the opportunity to respond to the question for as soon as Dad spoke those last words the baby started kicking hard and the contractions began at a minute apart. I found a chair and sat down to catch my breath. Everyone around me was enjoying the evening in its fullest; unaware of what was happening to me.

We celebrated the arrival of the New Year in full force. To my surprise my water broke around 12:30 in the morning. I waddled into the bathroom and called out to anyone who would hear me. If anyone has ever attended a Puerto Rican celebration, you would understand how difficult it was to break up the party.

My Mom and oldest sister came to my rescue. They drove me down to Serra Memorial Hospital in Sunland, California. We arrived at one o'clock on New Year's morning. After checking in I was immediately admitted and wheeled into a room. My pregnancy was an easy one. I was very blessed. Morning sickness never affected me. As I laid in bed waiting for the nurse to prepare me before surgery, I dozed off. When I awoke, I noticed my mother sitting in the room with me. I have always had a high tolerance for pain, so when a contraction hit, I didn't scream.

My mother, however, was not aware of my tolerance threshold. One should always respect the advice given by one's mother, no matter how old one is. Holding my hand she advised me to scream on the next contraction. "Let it out girl... it will help you with the pain," she said. I looked at her and shook my head and responded with "Ok mom...I will". I was so tired from the party I kept dozing in and out of consciousness. Mom was standing next to my bed when the next contraction hit. I let out the loudest scream possible. I mean why wouldn't any good daughter listen to her mother's request...right? Well, can you just imagine what happened next. As soon as I screamed, my mother fainted! Incredible! My oldest sister just happened to walk into the room while I was screaming and low and behold she was able to catch Mom before she hit the floor! I was amazed that Mom reacted that way. It wasn't funny at the time, but it brings back fond memories when I think of it now.

I was awoken at 1:30 in the morning to be wheeled into the delivery room. The bed on wheels was brought into the surgical room and as close to the operating bed as possible. The staff asked me to move myself over from one bed to the other. What caught my attention was the gap between the two beds. I shared my concern about the gap with the nurses and ask them to close the gap between the two beds.

Not only was I in labor but now I had to concern myself with my safety. The nurses closed the gap. I maneuvered myself onto the surgical bed, when both my feet went into spasms. "Great," I thought, what else can happen? The nurse came around and started to rub my feet to ensure the spasm sensations would cease before I was given the anesthesia, which I gladly accepted. It was 3:55 in the morning when I delivered a healthy beautiful baby boy. Daniel arrived a whopping seven pounds three and one-half ounces, twenty one inches long. My son was born on New Year's Day morning in the year of our Lord 1979.

I was advised by the nurse on the morning shift of how the night shift nurses were unable to wake me. I must have been more tired than I thought. The nurses decided to let me sleep and were kind enough to feed the baby while I slept. I slept a whole twenty-four hours! January 2nd was the first time I held Daniel in my arms. My eyes swept over his tiny body; he was so beautiful. What a gift!

I was given a clean bill of health and was released from the hospital on January 3rd, my birthday. That same night, I was settling in for the evening when there was a knock on the door. Wesley came by to see the baby before heading out to Okinawa on his next assignment. He was allowed to spend the night to spend time with Daniel. I drove him to LAX the next morning. We said our goodbyes. I have always made it my guiding principle never to look back on relationships. If I dwelled on what

I had, I'd miss out on the future. Holding onto my principles, I made it a point not to have any further communication with him. All was going well until one day I went down to the mail box to pick up the mail. One envelope caught my eye. It was an invitation. "Who would be sending me an invitation," I thought. Opening it, I read it and to my surprise it was an invitation sent to me by the woman whom, Wesley was seeing while we were married. It was an invitation to their wedding. I felt the knife of infidelity pierce my heart once again as it did before. In an instant I despised him for allowing her to send me that invitation.

I was raised to believe that marriage was a sacred union between a man and a woman. I went into my marriage believing in those values. In spite of everything, even though I tried without success to save my marriage, I left the union full of guilt, shame and blamed myself for its failure.

Second Marriage - Edwardo

Several months after my Daniel's birth, I met my girlfriend's cousin. At first, Edwardo was caring and hardworking and was willing to accept an already made family. Little did I know the type of individual he truly was! Although we loved each other throughout the years, his drinking brought out the worst in him. The more he drank the more abusive he became.

The first incident occurred in 1982. We were renting a house with my parents in North Hollywood. It was a warm summer night when a discussion turned into a heated argument. I am unsure as to why the argument started in the first place. Screaming was the precursor to fighting between us. The fight then moved into the bedroom where Edwardo closed the door and locked it behind him.

The fights were always physical in nature. Edwardo believed the only way to win the arguments was through physical abuse. The argument increased in intensity. The harder I tried to get away, the meaner he became. He grabbed me by my throat, slammed me down onto the bed and with both hands started to choke me. I can still feel his hands on my neck, slowly choking the life out of me. I must have passed out for I was unable to recall anything else that happened until I regained consciousness. I opened my eyes and grasped for air while he was shaking me awake. I managed to get up and out from under his grip, my hand clutching my throat. He looked at me - his face pallid. He sat there repeating over and over again how much he regretted what just happened and how much he loved me; promising to never allow it to happen again. Still clutching my throat, my eyes the size of saucers in disbelief, I slowly backed away from him heading towards the door. Turning the bolt as quietly as I could, I unlocked the door and ran out leaving him to stew in his expressed grief.

It is during this point in an abusive relationship when women fall into the trap. Love for our husbands is the forgiving element which keeps us trapped in the vicious cycle. My self-esteem began to dwindle when I started to believe it was my fault he retaliated the way he did. If I wasn't such a bad wife he could then feel worthy of me. Trying to fix what I considered was wrong kept my self-esteem plummeting onto the negative side of the scale. Blind love seized me and kept from making the mistake of being the one to ruin my marriage by convincing me to stay within the abusive relationship. My thoughts became reliant on my relationship. Thoughts such as "How would I be able to support myself and my son?" "How would I survive?" Lacking one's self-worth gives rise to self-doubt. Whether I upheld a great job, did not matter. Living under the controlling thumb of another individual only gave rise to the fear of the unknown and caused me to remain in the clutches of my abusive relationship.

As my marriage grew into years, the abuse grew more frequently. The more we fought, the more I tried to reason with myself, and the more I convinced myself the blame was all mine. "I failed at my first marriage," I thought, "I was not intent on blowing this one as well." I immersed myself into the marriage to make it work, no matter the cost. So as months turned into years, the more I convinced myself to endure the abuse.

Summer arrived in California and on this particular summer day it was blistering. Of course, the air conditioning in the car decided not to work. Traffic was unbearable as I was driving home after picking up Daniel from preschool. When we arrived home, I rushed upstairs to change our soaked clothes. A few minutes later Edwardo walked in. He looked angry. Since I was accustomed to that look, I learned it best to leave him alone. Being straightforward, I told him that I was not in the mood to talk or argue. In reality all I wanted was time to cool down from the heat and the drive home before starting dinner. He would not hear of it. "Please, just leave me alone," I said. I'd had enough of his arguing with me in front of Daniel. Nothing I said would appease him. He was determined to argue with me even though I asked him not to. He started in on me.

The argument became heated. We were now face to face screaming at each other when he started to throw punches. I raised my arms to defend myself. Even with that he managed to get me into a head hold. What could I do? I had to think of a way to get out from under his grip. He held my head down between his legs. Looking at his feet the opportunity to escape presented itself. I jumped on the opportunity, not wasting any time. My adrenalin was pumping! My survival instincts kicked into gear and my hand went up and grabbed his genitals. I can only describe my grip as that of a bulldog. I pulled on his genitals as hard as I possibly could until he released me from his grip. Daniel hearing the fight came out into the living room to watch us...crying.

When Edwardo released his grip on me, I ran over to Daniel, snatched him up and ran out the front door heading down the hall to my girlfriend's apartment praying she'd be there. I got to her door and banged on it! "Linda are you there?" "Please be there!" I said. Linda opened the door and Daniel and I ran inside. "Lock the door...please," I told her. I was so grateful she was home. Since Edwardo had guns in the house all I could think about was him chasing after us with a gun ready to kill us. Thirty minutes went by when we heard a bang on the door.

My adrenalin was still rushing threw my veins, when Linda opened the door. I walked over to the door, noticing he was carrying something in his hand. I looked down. He thrust his hand at me and I noticed the towel was full of blood…his blood. "See what you did…now I have to go to the hospital." "GO to the hospital, you started the fight anyway. You deserved it," I shouted back. I could only surmise the blood was discharged from his penis after our fight. He stood at the door for a few more seconds expecting an apology. An apology would not be forthcoming. He turned around, and walked away. I closed the door and returned to the kitchen to finish my visit with Linda. Edwardo never apologized for starting the fight.

I did learn, however, what truly happened to make him angry. The story was that sometime during the day when the receptionist was on the phone with her husband and unbeknownst to Edwardo, he began flirting with her. The receptionist's husband heard Edwardo's flirtatious innuendos on the other end of the line and became enraged. He rushed down to the law office where Edwardo worked, asked for Edwardo and when Edwardo greeted him, punched him out cold.

When Edwardo regained consciousness he was humiliated and outraged from what had occurred. The only way he could secure his manhood was to take his frustrations out on me. He left his office irate and looking for a fight. Thinking he would meet with a submissive wife when he arrived home, he was sadly mistaken. When the ultimate arbiter of his choices and actions were his feelings he allowed himself to be swept by those feelings and encountered defeat. God was once again watching over Daniel and I.

After many years of abuse, I tried to regain my dignity and self-esteem by trying to leave Edwardo. In trying to put my affairs in order, I went to court and filed for a restraining order. I left the court house and arrived early at Daniel's preschool, parking the car in front as I usually did. Entering the preschool I located Daniel's teacher to inform her of the situation. I gathered all of Daniel's things and headed out the door. I had just opened the car door for Daniel when Edwardo came around the side of the school building, rammed a gun into my ribcage and shoved us into the car. He ordered me to drive. Daniel was in the back seat unaware of what was truly going on. Edwardo's jealously and controlling traits began to take over his demeanor. "Get in the car!" he said. I had no reservations about his intentions of killing us if I were to leave him. I had to try. Edwardo sat in the passenger seat pointing the gun at me. "It's a good day to die," he said. My thoughts were only of Daniel sitting in the back seat. How was I going to get us out of this? "Daniel, sweetie…put on your seatbelt, ok?" "Yes, Mami," he said. Then a thought hit me.

My foot hit the gas and the car shot out onto the street. My foot felt like a heavy weight as I continued accelerating the speed of the car. I began to laugh uncontrollably. I turned my face and looked at Edwardo and said "Ok then WE WILL ALL DIE!" The car was racing down the street at a high speed. I began to drive irrationally swerving in and out of traffic, hoping my plan would put fear in Edwardo. It did! I turned again to look at him. His facial features turned from menacing and vicious to one of fearing for his own life. I looked in the rear view mirror and said to Daniel, "Hold on baby." My foot hit the brake pedal hard as I brought the car to a rubber burning stop. "GET OUT!" I shouted as I reached over him and opened the door. Shocked, Edwardo still in a daze fell out of the car. I grabbed the passenger side door, slammed it shut and hit the gas and drove off leaving him on the side of the street, stunned. If it wasn't for the mighty hand of God and His intervention, Daniel and I would not have been spared.

Women under the threshold of fear tend to blame themselves for the situation they are in, I know I did. Becoming more attentive, asking myself what can I change to make my relationship better or how can I become a better wife? My self-esteem was non-existent, feeling worthless; I placed the full weight of blame and guilt on my shoulders. Not until many years later did I realize the problem was not with me, but with

Edwardo. There was no sense of balance. On one hand I was trying to analyze why my marriage was deteriorating, on the other desperately trying and without success, to hang onto my relationship.

After all the struggles and hardships, I was faced with the fact that my husband was having an affair with a co-worker named Genna, a married woman. At first, I was unaware of their relationship. It became apparent when he invited Genna and her husband and kids over for dinner. As time went by he began to see her more and more.

Finding out about the affair was devastating, so I confronted Edwardo. He promised to break it off with her, saying "It was a temporary fling," while pleading for another chance. What was I to do? I weighed the pros and cons seeking a resolution; my desire was not one for discarding twelve years of marriage. I agreed to provide him a second chance under one condition, temporary separation. I decided to lease a small apartment temporarily in hopes a separation would be the glue needed to bring about a final reconciliation. Although he professed to love me and promised to terminate his affair with Genna, he continued to deceive me. The affair continued for many months after his promise of fidelity. He invited Genna into our home and slept with her in our marriage bed, defiling the sanctity.

Dreams have always been an integral part of my life. So one night as it happened, I had a dream. I dreamt that Genna was pregnant. The next morning when Edwardo came to visit, I asked him to sit down. I was too anxious to sit, so I decided the best thing to do was to pace back and forth. "I had a dream last night," I said. Entering into my discourse explaining in detail what the dream entailed. I stopped pacing, turned to him, and pointed a finger at him. "She's pregnant is she not," I asked bluntly. He was shocked! He looked at me in amazement. His mouth dropped open and he stared at me in disbelief. I allowed a moment for my words to sink in. As I studied his face, it was obvious his mind was working and processing the information he had just received. He said "But…how can you know, she is going to the doctor today to confirm it." "Well she is," I said. "Genna will be calling me later in the evening with the results," he said. "I don't need to know. Just please leave," I said. Edwardo slowly raised himself off the chair and with his head lowered walked out of the apartment. I felt my heart drop into the pit of my stomach. "Why was this happening again? Was I destined for a life of infidelity, and sexual immorality?"

We have these preconceived notions that God wants us to remain in an abusive and unfaithful relationship in order to save a marriage. Yes, God is in favor of marriages staying intact for He hates divorce (Malachi 2:16). But with that in mind, I tried many times and on many occasions to work on keeping our marriage together, however, in the end it remained a one sided agreement. God does allow a wife to seek divorce for marital unfaithfulness (Matthew 19:9). God is a loving, merciful; gracious, long-suffering and abounding in goodness and truth (Exodus 34:6).

So why is it then one believes that one has to stay in an abusive and unfaithful relationship? "You are worthless. You failed in your marriage. You are lousy at your job. See, you can't even balance a check book. Your kids don't love you. Go ahead take another drink. No one cares about you anyway." Our thoughts are manipulated by the evil one who enjoys making us feel unworthy. Satan will use all trickery and all treachery known to him to keep us from the wonderful plan God has for us. I know full well what it is to do battle. When Jesus walked the earth, he was a peaceful man. A man through His goodness healed the lame, the blind, the sick and raised people from the dead. He was the Son of Man.

Many times we walk day by day thinking everything is fine, wearing a façade, giving an overall impression to others that our lives are fine. I have been one to give the impression that my life was all peaches and cream. In reality it was not. Nevertheless, I was incapable of changing my situation, as I believed my destiny was to suffer. How was I to know that a life of peace, love and harmony existed outside of the one I was living? I was unable to fathom happiness as a way of life when in the midst of turmoil. My daily thoughts were to preserve the sanity and maintain a solid foundation for my son. My choices, unbeknownst to me, would ultimately affect my future and my son's future.

I managed to acquire a little apartment in Palmdale, about half a mile south of Main Street on a hill. The apartment allowed me to get away from a difficult situation. I was angry and over wrought. I wallowed in my grief and guilt.

Going through the emotional ride was devastating especially since I had to go through it alone, or so I thought. It was during this painful season I met a young woman by the name of Missy. My apartment complex was designed to accommodate two apartments on the second floor accessible by one staircase. My neighbor, Sue had two children. Her children at times would play with Daniel. During great weather days my neighbor Sue and I would keep our doors opened while the kids ran back and forth chasing each other. One day I walked into Sue's apartment to visit. Missy, a hair stylist was visiting and cutting Sue's hair. We began to talk and instantly we both knew it was the beginning of a friendship. Our friendship flourished and developed into a relationship closer than sisters, we became the best of friends. Because of the wonderful bond I developed with Missy, I was able to face what was to befall me. Missy was an amazing angel sent by God to provide support, comfort, as well as alleviate some of the pain associated with separation and divorce.

Edwardo was not the type of man to live alone while trying to reconcile his marriage. He had moved into an apartment with Genna located in the San Fernando Valley some thirty miles away. He called me after his last visit to share with me the fact that she was pregnant. "Her intentions are not to keep it," he said. "Why are you telling me this? I don't want to know anything about it," I said and hung up. Several days later he called me again to inform me of Genna's abortion. For some unknown reason, instead of Edwardo and Genna retreating to their apartment after her appointment, Edwardo decided to rent a room at a motel located on Main Street, half a mile from my apartment complex. Leaving Daniel with Sue, I drove down the hill to the motel. Entering the motel office I acquired the room number from the manager. The motel was a square shaped building with all the rooms facing an interior courtyard. I left the motel office and calmly located the room in which they were staying. Taking a deep breath, I walked over to the door. The curtains were closed, yet I could still see Genna through a small gap at the end of the curtain. Genna was lying on the bed, pain reflecting on her face as anguish pressed down on her brows.

I banged on the door and yelled for Edwardo to open up. "I know you're in there," I said. I moved away from the door and peered again through the gap in the curtain and I saw her frightened face as she knew who it was. I banged louder and louder and screamed for him to open the door. "I know you're in there!" I said, profanity spewing from my lips. I turned and noticed several people coming out of their rooms to observe what was going on. The door was finally opened. I hastily walked in pushing Edwardo deeper into the depths of the room. He was drunk, trying to wash away his misery in a bottle of Bacardi. He understood and was aware of his sinful disposition.

I was now face to face with Edwardo. He lowered his eyes since he was incapable of meeting mine. I snatched the bottle of Bacardi away from him and began to pour it all over his head. He just stood there rocking back and forth in his drunken stupor accepting his fate; the alcohol dripping from his hair onto his face, down onto his clothes, entirely drenching him. I looked over at Genna quietly lying on the bed. She was balled up like a little girl, her arms wrapped around her knees. "Good," I said. She won't give me any problems. My face turned once again to Edwardo. He just stood there...drunk. He knew I was angry; obscenities continuously spewing out of my mouth while I depleted the remainder of the Bacardi rum all over him. I lowered the empty bottle and let it slip out from my fingers onto the floor. He stood there, unmoved. My hand went into my jean pocket and withdrew my cigarette lighter. I flicked the lighter on, hearing a low gasp..."Ah" from behind me.

I stared him down, screaming…"How dare you do this to me? How dare you have an affair, get her pregnant in our home and in our bed? My God, why did you allow another woman to enter our sanctuary and destroy our marriage? I gave you the best years of my life! Answer me," I yelled. I was so focused on Edwardo I was oblivious to the world around me. I noticed the lighter was still flickering in my hand. Just then I noticed my hand moving slowly towards the man who, for many years physically and mentally abused me. How desperately I wanted to bring an end to those memories of unhappiness bestowed upon me by this man.

Instantly, I had one thought; a thought which wiped out all other thoughts. Only one word was spoken to my inner mind. The word was "Daniel." It was that thought which brought me back from insanity to my full senses and out of the possessed state of revenge I was currently in. Immediately I stopped. Released the lighter, lowered by hand, placed the lighter in my pocket and took a step back.

I turned and looked at Genna, her face still in shock lying on the bed. I returned my gaze to Edwardo and said in a loud voice "You two deserve each other. I won't waste any more time on either of you!" I turned and walked over to the door, opened it and stepped out slamming it behind me. Outside, I took a deep breath and thanked God for saving me from doing something I would regret for the rest of my life. I returned home praying and thanking God for his intervention. On this day and at this particular crossroad I chose a better life for me and my son. I returned home to the open arms of my beautiful son, Daniel.

The incident left me so unprepared for the amount of guilt, pain, depression and emotional hurt associated with a twelve year relationship. Edwardo ceased harassing and calling me two years after our confrontation. The healing process was able to commence only after the calls ended.

Third Marriage – Paul

They say three times is a charm. Yet three times was not for me. This relationship was slightly different from the first two in two ways. My first two husbands were Puerto Ricans, jealous, controlling and physically abusive. My third husband was Caucasian and although he was not physically abusive towards me, he enjoyed manipulation through psychological competitiveness or head games. I regard mental abuse as damaging as physical or emotional abuse.

We were married on July 4, 1992 in Las Vegas. Soon after, I noticed changes within our relationship developing. The changes were minor at first, but were becoming more apparent. I decided to discuss my concerns with Paul. Although they were minor, Paul looked at me and told me not to worry. His said "He was going through a phase and needed to become accustomed to being married." "Ok," I said and gave him the benefit of the doubt.

Several months went by and Paul came to me to discuss his desire of relocating closer to his mother and stepfather in West Virginia. Problems in his youth forbade him from developing a great relationship with them. This was his way of atoning for his past heartlessness. I agreed to share a life with him and on April 1, 1993 we packed up all our belongings and made our way east. I have heard the aphorism "People do not change." I will distinctly contradict that statement. It has been my experience that certain types of men prefer to display a mask of pretense while hiding behind a façade of deceit, dishonesty and self-centeredness when it relates to gain.

Whatever emotional and loving tendencies Paul had while we were dating disappeared upon taking the vows of marriage. I began to see aspects of his personality come to light with each passing day. Trying to help him develop into a better person through positive reassurances of his abilities, were simply rejected. He carried a large chip on his shoulder. The whole world was indebted to him. He refused to see it any other way.

Refusing to appreciate his family or consider a change in his paradigm only preserved his resentment towards life. This kept fueling our disputes, arguing constantly about our finances. The longer hours I worked to provide the support my family required, the less he assisted in supporting us. Obviously he decided he had free reign on our checkbook. Settling one debt only gave rise to two others. Working long hours trying for many years to keep my family out of debt, fighting constantly, I lost the battle. Feeling betrayed I had no other choice than to file for bankruptcy against my better judgment. Filing for bankruptcy did not have an effect on Paul whatsoever; yet it was devastatingly so for me.

Believing I would find some emotional reprieve after we filed never materialized. I maintained a stringent work schedule leaving early in the morning and arriving home late in the evenings. Anything to keep me distracted from daily contact with Paul. My unhappiness, suspicions and anxieties grew steadily. So much so, it began to affect my relationship with Daniel. Observing the strife it created on my relationship with my son, grieved me. The love for my son was greater than the love for my husband who refused to recognize or acknowledge his responsibility of provider, husband, father or friend. Year after year I prayed for God's intervention in Paul's life. I prayed for him during the day, and I prayed over him while he was asleep; hoping beyond hope for God to transform him. Time was my nemesis.

Prayer was an avenue I continued to work through to find relief from a life of regret and failure. Gradually thoughts of Phoenix began to emerge. The anticipation of embarking on a new life instigated fervent enthusiasm within my very existence. Carrying the burden of agonizing worry, sleeplessness, sorrow, and struggling within a loveless marriage for countless years, was the medium by which I approached God to ask for some measure of peace for my miserable life. The peace only a magnificent God could provide. No matter what the future had in store for me. He responded and I felt the peace, assurance and guarantee of the promise given to me by the Almighty God of a wonderful new future. In faith I began to research, organize and arrange my plans to relocate to Phoenix.

One day Paul came by my office to convey the fact of a communiqué he received from a company in Ohio to whom he submitted his resume. "They want to interview me," he said. "But there is one catch. I have to drive to Ohio for the interview." "Really…when are you leaving?" I responded in shock. "I'm leaving tonight after I pack a bag," he said. Our relationship up until that point was merely formal. Paul was simply advising me of his intended departure. Discussions, conversations or communication were rare, few and far between. Our relationship was strictly platonic and civil at best. Paul departing was a welcomed relief. It was Friday afternoon when he left my office and headed home, packed a suitcase and drove off to Ohio in my BMW. The very fiber of my being screamed "Hooray!" "At long last I would be able to enjoy some peace and quiet," I thought. I looked forward to thoroughly enjoying the solitude of a weekend without him.

A weekend turned into a week without any communiqué from Paul. I became worried. He carried a pager with him so I tried paging him. The pager had been disconnected. Unsure of what, if anything happened to him, I contacted Sue, his mother in West Virginia. My friendship with Sue increased over my seven years of marriage to Paul. "Sue," I said. "Have you heard from Paul?" "No…why?" she replied. "Well…," I said and began to recount in detail what transpired. She listened tentatively. Struggling to comprehend and rationalize the reason for Paul's blatant behavior was arduous. "What do we do now," she asked. "Well…there is nothing we can do. We will have to wait and see if either of us hears from Paul," I said.

When Paul checked in several days later, his voice was harsh and abrasive. Apparently he had spoken to his mother. "Why did you call Mom? Why were you checking up on me?" he screamed. "For the same reason any wife would…I was worried," I replied. "Since you were incapable of providing me with an address or phone number in case of an

31

emergency, I was concerned. Paul, why are you angry? Are you hiding something?" I asked. "Don't lie to me Paul! You always change the subject when you are lying," I yelled back. Our discussions always culminated into heated arguments. We were both stubborn and unwilling to concede to the other. Compromise was a distant memory. Paul developed a distinguishing characteristic which he perfected throughout the course of our marriage. Since Paul enjoyed driving, he frequently used the phone to manipulate our conversation. I called it his conversation manipulation technique. Knowing instinctively the direction our conversation was headed, I ended the call.

There is nothing anyone can say to contradict my belief that God dispenses the right amount of support at the precise moment it is needed through an Angel wrapped up neatly in a package called -"friend." Friends encourage, comfort and helps us to endure and triumph over what one has to embark upon. Ron was such an individual. For many years our friendship was merely as acquaintances. Yet several months before Paul's escapade, Ron and I became great friends.

Paul was still away from home, occasionally calling to ensure I had not moved. Peace enveloped the house while he was away. The intense friction permeating the interior of the house slowly melted as the days grew into weeks. My heart hoped that he would never return. I looked forward to the Memorial Day weekend as a welcomed change from the daily work grind. I invited Ron over for a BBQ to celebrate and remember those who gave us our freedom. Ron and I were hovering over the BBQ, enjoying a day filled with sunshine, a faint breeze and the smells of a variety of meats simmering over a hot mesquite grill when we both turned around and saw a tanned Paul standing at the back door. My heart sank.

Apparently Paul's conversation manipulation technique suffered defeat; overthrown by my strong resolve in a victorious crush. He despised losing dominion over me and returned home to reclaim it. Instantly I heard the crackling and felt the static charge in the air. The joy I felt just minutes before was now overshadowed by his dark presence. My body instantly reacted to his unwelcomed arrival. Ron and I tried to make the best of his arrival by asking Paul to share in the merriment of the day. Paul remained in the house unwilling to participate or socialize. We made the best of the remainder of the day and after several hours Ron took his leave.

During the summer months in Virginia, the humidity always brought showers, so I made it a habit to watch the weather forecast nightly. Interestingly enough Ohio was under a storm watch for the preceding three weeks. Remember, Paul indicated he was driving to Ohio for an interview. Ohio did not see a break in the rain for the last three weeks. "Hum"…I thought. I walked up to Paul, cast my eye over him and inquired "How did you get so tan?"

An individual who propagates lies tends to experience a sense of entrapment and immediately becomes defensive when confronted with the true facts. His facial expression was indicative of that. Scrambling for an answer, his demeanor was disingenuous. His eyes were incapable of meeting mine. I waited for a response and after a few moments, I said "Well?" Not expecting such a confrontation, he muttered and said "After work I go home and sit outside with a sun reflector." "Really…that must be difficult," I said, "As it's been raining for the past three weeks in Ohio!" Glaring at him, I walked away, leaving him dumbfounded.

The house we rented was a small three bedroom house. The rooms connected by a small hallway. The following afternoon, we crossed paths in the hallway. Paul walked out of the master bedroom as I was walking in. I looked down and in his right hand was the small ring case which stored our original set of wedding rings. "What may I ask are you doing with the ring case?" "What?" he said. "Our original ring set. Oh, I see… you are going to take the rings with you and present it to your new found girlfriend?" "No…what makes you think that?" he asked. "Yea, right… whatever," I said and continued into the room. This was only one of many quandaries Paul took pleasure in. A life geared for self-indulgence and self-destruction.

At last the long weekend came to an end. With his belongings packed, Paul was ready to depart to wherever he was going, without providing an address or phone number. His reason being for the lack of contact information was that "Since his company provided him with living arrangements, he was unable to disclose the information." "My goodness," I said. What incredible nonsense. Did he expect me to buy that?

Paul had made the decision to leave his home in order to test the waters. The increase in turmoil, the numerous arguments and threats resulted in both of us growing in dissatisfaction and emptiness. Paul decided to take the initiative to end our marriage, despite the fact that he continued to have a sense of dependency on our relationship through his manipulative tendencies. A part of his inherit character.

Several weeks after the Memorial Day weekend, I arrived home from work, parked the car and walked outside to the mail box to collect the mail. There was nothing special in the mailbox, just the regular monthly bills along with one or two pieces of junk mail. I stood outside breathing in the fresh air. "What a lovely evening," I thought. Turning from the mailbox, I went inside the house, walked through the living room and into the kitchen. Dropping the mail on the counter, I went into the bedroom to change into my comfy clothes before starting dinner. Removing the day's stress and feeling more or less normal, I strolled into the kitchen, picked up the mail and began sorting through them. The first envelope I opened was the phone bill. My mouth dropped as I stood there bewildered. My face reflecting a look of shock and horror as my eyes stared at the amount due. The total was a whopping $849.00 for one month of calls. I was beside myself, unaware that I was screaming. Who in their right mind could personally talk for a total of $849.00 dollars worth of service!

I was furious. Then I began to cry. How was I ever going to pay for this? "My God, what had I done to deserve this?" I was standing in the kitchen…balling. My hands were to my side, my head flopped down, shoulders sagging, eyes closed…crying. I could not contain myself.

34

Introduction

Something inside me snapped. It was like the dam in my heart broke and a flood of tears came pouring out. I walked out the kitchen, down the hallway to my bedroom, tears blinding me. My body felt numb. I climbed into bed, curled myself into a fetal position and cried myself to sleep. Why was I chosen to deal with such a barrage of pain, guilt and hurt? It was more than I could bear.

Several days had elapsed before my mind allowed me to deal with the issue of the enormous phone bill. I began to scan all the numbers to see if I could find a random pattern. There was! The bill was littered with numerous calls to one number in Florida. What could I do? There was no other way. I had to face it head on. My hand gripped the receiver; my fingers slowly punching in the numbers. The phone began to ring, once... twice, and just as I was about to hang up, a boy answered. There was no backing out now. "Hi," I said. "In going through my phone bill I found numerous calls to this number. Can you tell me who I am calling?" The boy responded "Hi I'm Jeff." "Hi Jeff, may I speak to your mom?" "Sure," he said and asked me to hold on while he went to get Natalie. "Ok girl, try to keep yourself calm," I thought.

I felt as though time had stopped, for it seemed like an eternity before Natalie came to the phone. "Hello," Natalie said. "Hi, my name is Jenny Fisher and I was hoping you could give me some information as to why your number appears on my phone bill." "Fisher," she said. "Yes, that is correct," I responded. Immediately she began to divulge everything that had occurred since Paul's arrival to Florida several months before. The truth was finally brought to light. Paul was having an affair with Sherry, Natalie's daughter, whom Paul met over an internet chat room. He fabricated the story of working in Ohio in order to create a diversion to voyage down to Florida. Jeff, Sherry's brother was listening in on the other receiver when he declared, "I told you Mom - I knew there was something not right with Paul!"

Natalie went on to say, Paul called Sherry numerous times a day. They were constantly conversing and it was during one of those conversations wherein Paul asked Sherry to marry him. Upon Paul's arrival in Florida, he stayed in Natalie's home. A month or so later Paul and Sherry along with Sherry's daughter moved into a motel room, and they were currently living in the motel at the time of my call. Left to himself Paul was a smooth talker, pretending to be single he lied for self gain, despite the fact we were still married.

Natalie, her suspicions aroused, began to ask questions. When she asked Paul where he worked, Paul purportedly stated he worked for the NFL. In spite of that alleged fact, he was never observed working. At this point I interjected and asked Natalie if she noticed Paul with a box containing a set of wedding rings. "They were our first set," I said. "Yes," she said. "Paul took them to the jewelers and had them sized for Sherry." Unbelievable! How could Paul be so disrespectful?

Natalie was joyously vocalizing how she came across a picture of Paul standing beside a woman and a child, twenty minutes into the conversation. She inquired about it and Paul responded "oh, that's my sister with my nephew." Listening to specific details of the last few months was becoming more and more unhealthy. My breathing was becoming erratic. Hearing those words spoken pierced my heart. I was riding the emotional roller coaster once again. My unanticipated call provided the avenue by which Natalie amusingly exposed the startling truth. It gushed out like a seven story tsunami intending to kill.

Natalie was not giving up. Her distrust in Paul was her driving force to attain as much information on him as possible. "So I asked him who the registered owner of the BMW was?" she said. "I knew he was lying when he responded that the vehicle was registered to his mother." Natalie's intention was to discredit Paul at all costs. I was too stunned… no…flabbergasted. My heart was breaking and I was unable to withstand any more pain. I said goodbye to Natalie and hung up. Shaking uncontrollably I began to cry hysterically.

Was this ever going to end? My life was filled with broken promises…broken vows. I never understood why promises were so easily broken. I needed to clear my head. Time…I needed time to compose myself. My entire body was under emotional distress and torment. Feeling so alone in the dark recesses of my room, I picked up the receiver and called Ron. Friends are such a comfort when dealing with such news. I was grateful for such a friend. His gentle and loving soul always helped to calm me. Feeling much better I said goodbye to Ron.

Paul was so incredibly easy to read. I knew him better than he knew himself. It was almost time for him to call. Paul enjoyed having control of every situation even through the means of long distance. The phone rang. My adrenalin spiked. My heart raced. I took a deep breath, held it and then slowly released it. He was punctual to say the least. Picking up the receiver I said "Hello," as naturally as I could. He was unaware of my conversation with Natalie earlier. Unable to stay calm, I blatantly asked "are you having an affair?!" An effective and powerful punch delivered through the means of communication. Can you imagine the shock! There was silence on the other end of the line, but only for a few seconds. He recovered almost immediately. When he finally spoke he denied it vehemently, saying "oh…I see. Who have you been talking too?" I know. "I'll get her for that!" "Paul," I said softly "For once in your life can you be honest with me and just admit the fact you are having an affair…please." "No…it is all a lie," he screamed. Attempting to keep my voice calm, I said "Do you remember what we promised each other when we first met?" No response, I was met with only silence on the other end of the receiver.

Our marriage was built on a foundation of shifting sand. Tired of his continuous excuses and lies I intentionally steered the conversation in a different direction by demanding the return of my car. "The car is registered to me. It is my responsibility," I said. "No." He adamantly refused. "Send me the money for the registration. The tags are going to expire," he said. "What do you think I am, Paul…stupid? I want the car returned to me within the next few days," and slammed the phone down on its cradle. "Lord," I said. "Is this ever going to stop?"

Furious I contacted the police and reported it stolen. The Police department contacted me several days later. A Detective Braddock was on the other end of the receiver. His speech was slow and precise. The following is what he recounted. "It appears someone attempted to drive-up to the DMV window to pay for your automobile registration," he said. "There were two people in the car, a man and a woman. The man handed a check to the clerk along with his driver's license. The check was signed by the woman who verbally identified herself as the owner of the vehicle...namely you. Since the car was reported stolen the plate appeared on the DMV's computers. The clerk immediately notified the police. In the meantime, trying to detain them the clerk declared to the pair that a problem arose with the system and asked if they could wait a little longer. Sensing something was wrong, the pair drove off in haste leaving the drivers license behind at the DMV window." Detective Braddock took a deep breath and said "Don't worry, they will shortly be apprehended. There is an APB out on the driver." "Please keep me advised," I said. I thanked him, I hung up.

Paul called me a few minutes later screaming and asking "Why did I report the car stolen." In a calm voice I said "Because I asked you to return the car to me, and you refused. In spite of that, you insisted on driving up to Virginia with Sherry and allowed her to forge my name and falsely identify herself as the owner of the car. What is the matter with you?!" I said. "Well, they can't get me – I'm already in North Carolina." Rolling my eyes, I slammed down the receiver.

I was contacted several hours later. "Mrs. Fisher?" "Yes," I said. "This is Detective Braddock." "What can I do for you...detective?" "We have your car. Paul and Sherry were captured trying to get out of the city. They were taken down to police headquarters." "What about my car," I asked. "It was moved to the impound yard, you can pick it up there. Do you want to press charges?" I thought for a moment, but before I could respond Braddock continued, "The purpose of my inquiry is to inform you that if you do press charges you may have to remain in Virginia until the case goes to trial, which may take several months or you may return on the day of the scheduled trial." "I'm sorry…detective, remaining in Virginia is no longer an option. Plans have already been finalized for my move to Phoenix in early August."

"Detective," I said. "Paul may remove whatever he can carry from the house. Once that has been achieved, please confiscate my house and car keys. I will be there within the hour." Saying farewell, I hung up. "Ok, this is not going to be easy," I thought. Scared of what I might do, I picked up the receiver and dialed Ron's number. "Hi Ron," I said and went into the details of all that had occurred. Ron agreed and drove from Virginia across town to Washington D.C., picked me up at my office and we headed back to Virginia. We were met by Detective Braddock when we arrived. Introductions aside, we walked down to the impound area discussing the case. "Paul and Sherry were escorted away from the house," he said. "They should no longer be a problem. Ah…here is your car." "Thank you…detective," I said. "Good luck in your future move." Handing over my keys, we shook hands and said our farewells. Ron and I walked around the car examining the exterior for any signs of damage. None were observed, so I started the car. I thanked Ron for being such a wonderful friend, an angel sent to me in my time of need and headed home.

Not wanting our conversations to degenerate into shouting matches, I decided the best course of action was to allow the answering machine to take the calls for the next several days. Paul made numerous attempts to communicate his frustration and sense of defeat through messages and his family, which all failed. This marriage was different as there were no memories of happy times. The dismal feeling of unhappiness was the cloud hovering over my seven year marriage. Memories of constantly fighting during the day while my pillows were tears stained at night overflowed my senses. Living through the experience of all the hurt and pain in my previous two marriages equipped me to be stronger and more independent of the dissolutions, disappointment and constant struggles within this marriage. We all know physical abuse is damaging both to the body as well as the mind. Mental abuse has the same ramifications as if it were physical.

Missy, my best friend came to stay with me with the intention of helping with the yard sales and the move. Time sped by like an unmanned freight train turning weeks into days until the day arrived for the move. Several days of yard sales were incredibly draining on all of us. Ron arrived at the house early to assist Missy and I load up the truck. Ron was kind enough to take time off, offering his services as a guardian angel to ride shotgun across country in the truck. Missy was elected to drive my car behind the truck. Everything packed, the house clean and locked, I got into the truck and started it up. Hooray! I began to have mixed emotions. I was headed towards a new destination, yet I was heartbroken as I was leaving my baby boy, Daniel behind. "Daniel will be fine," I thought. "You raised him independent and he will be able to take care of himself. So long baby," I said under my breath.

I said a short prayer. Pushing down slowly on the accelerator, the truck started to move. Driving the truck out of the driveway, my eyes filled with tears, I stuck my hand out of the window and waved goodbye to a life full of regret and broken dreams. "Thank you…Lord. Now I shall look forward to a wonderful new future." How exhilarating it felt to journey into the unknown where God was preparing the way for a life full of fresh new adventures.

Phoenix

When I decided to leave Virginia I was embarking on a new chapter in my life. I was moving to a strange city without any known family or friends. Nevertheless, I arrived in August 1998 and settled in Ahwatukee a suburb of Phoenix; carrying only the basic necessities. My first apartment was located in the Allegro Foothills Gateway. Attaining my apartment keys, from the manager, we drove around in search of my new home. The apartment was located on the second level across from the pool. Excitement stirred within me as I lifted my hand and inserted the key into the lock. The deadbolt slipped from its security position. My hand grabbed the knob and pushed the door open; I crossed over the threshold and into a new life. Standing at the entry gazing into what was to become my new life. Missy, Ron and I took a few moments to explore the apartment while stretching our legs before the start of the big job - unloading the truck. The temperature was a hundred and thirteen degrees that day. My skin felt as if the sun had placed a magnifying glass directly on me scorching my skin. Cold compresses were placed on our necks providing us with the necessary relief in order to complete the move without anyone fainting from heat exhaustion. My basic necessities consisted of a bed, a rocking chair, a small twenty-four inch television set to watch the outside world, my clothes and all the other nick-knacks one tends to acquire throughout one's life.

When we finished unloading the truck, exhausted from the trip, the heat and the physical labor we collapsed onto the floor to enjoy the coolness of the place. Sitting in the newness of my apartment, I thanked God for allowing my friends and me to make it to the new found land. Ron and Missy stayed with me for several more days before they returned home. We had a great time together. Saying goodbye was heartbreaking.

Being a constant workaholic, gave rise to an interlude of well deserved rest…a month of sheer relaxation. I'd get up at eight a.m. every morning, made breakfast and at ten in the morning went down and lounged at the pool until two in the afternoon, wherein I'd head back to the apartment, showered and took nap until four. Then I would head towards the on-site gym for my workout. I felt alive and free. Rediscovering what it meant to enjoy a life of leisure was what the doctor prescribed. Seizing the moment and enjoying a full month in which to recuperate provided my body the means to physically and mentally restore itself to health. Life was good until reality set in.

It was time for me to get back to work. After submitting dozens of resumes, I accepted a position with a property management company just to get my foot in the door. The position I accepted was no where compatible to the salary I received in Washington, D.C. After several months of struggling, it was apparent my finances were in dire straits. My financial difficulties did not deter me from executing a plan of acquiring an increased salary position. The first few years were arduous and extremely problematic. Nevertheless, I was determined to win at all costs and a challenge worth undertaking. Being left to fend for oneself, not only leaves a woman feeling inadequate, lonely, damaged but overall flawed. Three years later I was finally established in the property management field. My vocation began to consume most of my time thus substituting my inadequacies in its stead.

Although we are unable to see what is unfolding in our lives, God does. My life being as busy as it was became the focal point, while God slipped into second, third or even fourth position. The only time God was called upon was when I desired material possessions. You see, I had grown into a woman who idolized material things, although I was consciously unaware. When I felt lonely, my body immediately triggered the "Push the urge to shop," switch and it automatically kicked in, becoming my escape from loneliness. One night while doing my choirs I walked towards the kitchen and stopped at the counter. Looking up at the ceiling, I asked God to send me someone who loved me. I smiled and thanked him, not thinking about it again.

A relationship at this juncture in my life was out of the question, even though I asked God jokingly. I nudged forward towards my ultimate goal of achieving the American dream of owning a home. This time around I was focused on myself, and my future. Passion was my motivation. I could almost taste the sweetness of achievement. Then in an instant my dreams were gone, destroyed. The cause was that inevitable dreaded day of September 11, 2001. In January 2002 I was laid off and became one of many who suffered through and experienced the chilling aftermath of a struggling economy. I was devastated, yet I continued to ignore the God which helped me while I was in the mist of agony and despair during my last relationship.

One evening while watching a television program, the phone rang. I picked up the receiver and said "Hello." "Hi Mom," Daniel said. He began to explain what transpired in his life. The sluggish economy in California also affected the businesses, and left a lot of people unemployed. Unable to find further employment his solution was to contact me. It did not matter what was going on in his life, Daniel always had a home to return to, for as long as he needed. He always had a room waiting for him.

The excitement of my son returning home provided a new existence from the previous faded and drabbed outlook. We spoke for a few minutes longer before we hung up. My problems became minute and the overwhelming feeling of being unemployed no longer took precedence over my life. This time, my feelings were lifted. As I placed the receiver back on its cradle, my eyes veered once again to the ceiling as I said "God, I asked for you to send someone who loves me and although Lord that is not what I really meant, I thank you for it is an incredibly better gift." God's timing is always perfect.

Daniel was able to move in by the first week in March and I was able to find part time work in order to subsidize the income needed to assist with my financial responsibilities. Months went by and my inability to procure full time employment weighted heavily leaving me to maintain our existence off my savings. Surviving day to day for over seven and a half months was mentally and financially debilitating.

After many years of struggling through different seasons, failed marriages and chasing my own desires, I could no longer hold it together. In May 2002 I hit the lowest point in my life. I was broken! I was drowning, and going down for the final count. I was tired of struggling and endeavoring to do it all. My attempts were met with obstacles. In fact, life seemed as if it was progressively getting worse. "What was going on?

What had I done to deserve this?" I asked myself. One thing was for certain, I hastily opened a line of communication with God.

Unfamiliar with the aspects of prayer, I muddled through what I considered my first real conversation with God. How much more was I destined to endure? I had enough and was determined to convey my anger and disapproval to God. I sat down on my living room sofa and began to speak normally until I started to contemplate my struggles and everything I was currently experiencing. The tone in my voice began to increase its pitch. The more I thought about my dilemma, the more I screamed, yelled and thumped my feet. I was such an ungrateful child. I blamed God and held Him responsible for my demise, yet through it all, God remained patient and loving. Losing the ability to control my own life was devastating, demoralizing and degrading. How was I to know God's purpose for my life? I felt as though I was standing in quicksand unable to grab onto a life saving line. It was through this season God availed himself to me.

Sundays have always been a day I've allowed myself to sleep in. However, on one particular Sunday morning I woke up early and for some unknown reason I decided to put my hair in curlers. I had just finished my morning ritual when I walked into the kitchen. Daniel was already up when he walked in after me. He bent down and kissed my cheek; casually asking what my plans were for the day. I turned to look at him and said "I don't know…why?" "How about going with me to a new church I heard about?" he said. Pondering his question, I said "Sure, why not. I honestly don't have anything specifically planned for the day. Let me finish making breakfast first."

Making good or bad choices in the crossroads of life is what decides the outcome of one's tomorrow. Choosing to visit the church with Daniel on that Sunday morning was all God needed to start His life changing work in me. When God promises to be there for you, no matter what may arise, God never disappoints you or fails to keep His promises.

Introduction

Breakfast concluded we headed out. The drive was only fifteen minutes. As soon as I walked into the church foyer, I instinctively knew I had found the home I was looking for. I was received with opened arms. Everyone in the congregation was kind and welcoming. Sundays became a day I looked forward to. My desire to become a partner in the church groups opened up the opportunity and allowed me to serve in the youth ministry. In this capacity I was given the opportunity to become a big sister to six – eight year old girls. Daniel also flourished in his ministry working with the high school youths. Being able to work in the youth ministry on Wednesday nights was not only a privilege but also a blessing. If it were not for the incredible people in my life during my service in the youth ministry, and my passionate desire to enhance my life, the opportunity to share my story would not have been possible.

My life has revolved around my son. Striving hard to maintain a decent and positive environment for Daniel, while working long hours, only hindered my relationship with my precious son. At the same time, endeavoring to be both the mother and father figures, while providing for his life development and advancement, blinded me from the damage I caused through my absence. God's grace, however, intervened and although I lost those precious years, our relationship has strengthened and flourished.

I remember one Mother's Day in particular. I arrived at church like on any other Sunday and was greeted at the door. Crossing through the foyer, I headed into the sanctuary. Arriving early I was able to find my usual place, second row from the front, center. Pastor Lee began to speak. "This is a special Mother's Day," he said. "I would like to invite any one to come up to the microphone and share with everyone what your mother means to you." Sitting alone, I watched as one man went up, and then another and then another. How wonderful to witness the love those men displayed towards their mothers. I turned away for a moment, when I returned my gaze to the microphone I noticed Daniel walking towards the front of the sanctuary where the microphone was located. I observed a small gift and a rose in one hand while his other hand held a piece of paper containing a poem he wrote for this occasion. Standing in front of the entire congregation, he cleared his throat and began to read…

"Unconditional Love"

You gave me life
And sacrificed your own
To provide me with food,
Shelter and a quality home

🕷

As I sit and reflect
Your journey as a single mother
What I thought was neglect
Was just a Love like no other

🕷

You would do anything in your power
To shape and protect me
Even if that meant
Not knowing my daddy

🕷

I respect your decision
To be an independent woman
I understand your vision
To be there, because he wouldn't

🕷

Introduction

So here's what I've learned
And picked up through the years
That relationships are tough
And can make you shed tears

☒

No good comes from lies
It's what I understand
What woman needs a guy
If he's not willing to be a man

☒

Loyalty and Trust
Commitment and Faith
It's important to listen
And communicate each day

☒

Through sickness and in health
Whether poor, or gained wealth
Trials are painful
To prove we are faithful

☒

Life is confusing
And wisdom is essential
Courage is a strength that
Can maximize our potential

☒

JUST Rewards

Adrenaline will fluctuate
Emotions will rumble
Forgiveness is difficult
But we all must be humble

Love is an emotion,
That brings joy and fear
There is nothing like a bond
That's strong and sincere

From January to December
And each day of the year
I will always remember
That your love will be here

Whether near or far
Either happy or sad
I thank you for being
Both my Mom and Dad

I'll forever respect you,
And all that you've done
In my heart I call it
"Unconditional Love"
- Daniel Santiago

To my surprise, Daniel honored me as he stood in front of the congregation on that special Mother's Day. The sanctuary fell dead silent except for the light sobs. If a pin drop was to be heard that was the day it could be heard. Blinded by the tears flowing freely, I searched my purse for tissues. Having found none, my nose intentionally joined in on the free flow. Sniffling I tried to control my nose. Daniel finished reading his poem, smiled and asked me to come forward. Attempting to see, I stood up and walked towards him. Tears running down my eyes and nose, I knew my mascara was running. Standing beside him, Daniel presented me with a single red rose and a beautiful chain and cross, which he placed around my neck. He gave me a kiss and a big hug. Although I was oblivious to the congregation around me, I instinctly knew there was not a dry eye in the house of the Lord that day. My son honored me on that day, a day which will remain sealed in my heart for always.

How incredibly wonderful God is. No matter how painful the valleys were, God always shined a ray of hope in my direction.

Chapter Two
POWER OF PRAYER

Being part of the Youth Ministry was an experience I will always treasure. The ability to attend a service in the middle of the week provided the much needed mid-week boost which propelled me onward towards Sunday. Having to deal with seven months of part-time employment was extremely frustrating and left me feeling worthless.

God provided me with opportunities to immediately become acquainted with Him. You see in order for one to experience a conversation with God it has to be achieved through prayer. Prayer is the conduit that allows and enables one to build a personal relationship with God.

A baby, myself in Christian circles I needed to surrender my life in order to learn how to personally grow dependent on God. There was only one way for me to manage that and it was to learn how to express my feelings through the avenue of prayer. I began to realize that first and foremost, when one prays it is for the purpose of seeking God's will (1 John 5:14). After my futile and childish attempt to convey my disappointment to God; I began to understand that petitions for assistance, guidance, thanksgiving, adoration, praise, confession of sin or interceding, should always be asked in the name of Jesus. Prayer provides the ability for one's spirit to freely, openly and honestly express itself to God.

51

Wanting to become skilled at and gain the necessary knowledge on how to approach God through prayer; I surrounded myself and listened to those mature in their walk during Sunday service, small groups, and even Bible studies. Yet, when we accept Jesus Christ we are bestowed the gift of the Holy Spirit which abides in us and teaches us the will of God and helps us to pray. What an incredible partnership there is between the Holy Spirit and the human spirit. Through my prayer the Holy Spirit is able of finding the desire in the heart of the Father and then places the Father's desire in my heart.

God gives us the ability to receive the restoration of healing, truth, peace, cleansing and forgiveness (Jeremiah 33:6-8). My intention was to gain a discerning heart in order to recognize God's incredible character. To accomplish this I continuously recalled to mind that powerful prayer would only come from a clean heart. God does not hear us if we hold any malice in our hearts (Psalm 66:18). It is however, apparent that in today's society, many of us would rather hold onto our sins than enjoy true unbound and unrestrictive freedom of a prayer life that is unlimited.

Paradigms

Our lives are based on what we learn from our parents, and their parents. We have been raised to focus on ourselves. Growing up in our programmed life has taught us to be self-centered in our thinking while distorting our thoughts of money and relationships. My life was built on this premise. In order to win while ensuring my survival, self preservation was the norm. Developing self-centered thoughts only lead to my conviction that I had the power to control my own destiny. My attitude was one of vanity, self-centeredness, proudness, conceitedness and superiority. All the attributes I achieved through my life. The existence of a deity who created the heavens and earth (Genesis 1.1) was of no consequence. He was still unknown to me. Truth be known, I was indignant and incapable of releasing control of my life to anyone, much less to the God who created me in His own image (Genesis 1:27); or so I thought.

I had arrived at another cross road. After many years of struggling through abuse and infidelity, I became tired of the pessimistic, mundane, irreverence and the apparent futility of daily labor in my personal life. Is this all I am? Why is my pain unending? "God...there has to be more!" I screamed. Slowly I began to understand a change needed to be made to alter my paradigms or conditioning before I could begin to accept the blessings of God's abundance. It was during the lowest point in my life, broken, humiliated and at the end of my rope that I decided to allow God's sovereignty to rule over my life.

First I had to alter my method of traditional religious thinking, which reverts back to the old paradigm that poverty is a blessing. Those thoughts were driven by Satan. His only mission is to prevent, at all cost, the development of my personal relationship with God. For many, many years he kept me blinded from knowing God's provision, and always has been abundance. "How am I going to obtain such a transformation in my thought process?" I thought. Only one notion came to mind and that was to pray for deliverance from the hypocritical teachings on blessings of poverty. God's intention for anyone who accepts Jesus Christ as their Lord and Savior is to remove them from Satan's evil system of keeping everyone in poverty, blinded and in bondage (Isaiah 42:7).

Surrender

Choosing to surrender my mundane existence, and accepting Jesus Christ as my Lord, opened a gateway to freely allow God to mold me into a new creation. As difficult as it was to surrender without restraint, I had no other alternative. "Though we were spiritually dead because of the things we did against God, He gave us new life with Christ. You have been saved by God's grace," (Ephesians 2:5). Relenting my old ways was at first excruciating. Accepting the gift that God freely offered through his Son Jesus Christ was humbling.

Satan Attacks

I asked myself what would happen if I relinquished my life to God. How would I feel if I granted Him control of my life while renouncing my cares, worries and anxieties? Such contemplation was impacting my thoughts and the way I viewed my life. There was no doubt God would improve and enhance my existence better than I had thus far. So I decided to give Him a try. My soul was in turmoil. The interlude between the time I made the decision to let go and let God was like the thrashing of the restless seas. It was purely a spiritual warfare that I was experiencing. A tug of war was being fought between Satan, the treacherous thief, and my soul.

As God's calling became stronger within me, the tighter the clutches of Satan became. Romans 8:15 tells us that God did not give a spirit of fear. Why then is fear, anxieties, depression, sorrow, insecurities a constant struggle for all of us? It was the basic and fundamental tricks that were used as manipulative tools to keep me from taking the final step to the blessings that God longed to bestow upon me and which would take away the glory our Father so richly deserves. I needed to stay alert (1 Peter 5:8), for as soon as my thoughts drifted to a better future, the greatest enemy, the devil, began fervently pursuing me while trying to revert me back to my former behavior. Standing firm in the word and slowly growing strong in my faith was to arm and prepare me for the beginning of a new life.

Satan was relentless. Broken and depleted of all my resolve, I made the ultimate decision on May 17, 2002 at three o'clock in the morning. I humbly cried out to God and through the heart pounding sobbing cries, I surrendered wholeheartedly my life completely to and accepted my Lord and Savior Jesus Christ. Making the choice, released me from the sinful clutches that held me down. My decision was based on my strong conviction of a better future and away from my life based solely on a pandemonium of drugs, lies and unethical decisions.

Forgiveness

Forgiveness is a difficult subject to relate to. Emotions can be a powerful adversary or a fierce nemesis. My mind was dealing with so many questions. Why would God allow these things to happen to me? What had I done to deserve such injustice? Was I the victim of my circumstances or was God a vengeful God? Nothing made sense. My inability to comprehend left me feeling sick and resentful. Experiencing such ordeals kept me blinded and unforgiving. My mind was incapable of grasping the reality and overall truth of my situation.

Although I lacked knowledge in the omnipotent God, that fact did not concern me. My emotions were manipulating my thoughts by allowing me to focus only on how God abandoned and left me to face my predicaments alone. I found it incredibly difficult to deal with God. Why was I continuously crying out to Him? He never answered my prayers. Everything within me wanted to wholeheartedly understand.

When I asked, who am I Lord…that you would graciously offer me forgiveness? ***God responded:***

You…are my child.

▪ While I was drowning in my storms, were you there Lord?

    I…sustained you.

▪When I felt I could no longer hold onto life, and wanted so desperately to give up, were you there Lord?

    I…carried you.

▪ When I was being strangled into oblivion, were you there Lord?

    I…delivered you.

▪ When my son and I were forced into our car at gunpoint, were you there Lord?

    I…protected you.

▪ When I cried my eyes out, did you hear my sobs Lord?

I…wiped your tears away.

▪ When day after day looked bleak, were you there Lord?

    I…was your morning sun.

▪ When I cried out in pain after being beaten, were you there Lord?

    I…was healing your wounds.

▪ When my husbands' cheated on me, were you there Lord?

I...comforted you.

▪ When I drank myself into a stupor to help me make it through another night, were you there Lord?

I...held you.

▪ When my heart was broken numerous times and ached from lack of affection, were you there Lord?

I... loved you.

My struggle was and still is, as is for many - forgiveness. Did God expect me to forgive Him after the struggles and disappointments I dealt with all my life? No. It was accepting the fact that my choices placed me in the midst of those storms and trials, not God. Humankind was given the choice of free will. I was acquainted with right and wrong. Therefore, it was for me to ask for and accept God's grace forgiving me of my inequities. What an epiphany...understanding and accepting that simple fact. I made a promise to God when I accepted His Son Jesus Christ; and I was going to see it concluded.

Emotions are the source by which the evil one calls to us. Satan used my insecurities by means of my feelings in tempting me to take back control of my life. "No! Never," I said. This time conceding defeat and reverting back to my former habits was unfeasible and no longer acceptable. Since I was no longer inept, I had the capacity to alter my existence. Conforming to believing I was incapable and less than what God would have me believe of me and my abilities no longer restricted my talents.

It was a constant struggle as anxiety, worry and self doubt would always rear its ugly head. My desire to see the outcome of what God's purpose was for my life was the reminder of the promise and commitment I made to God. Since I considered myself lowly and unworthy and ashamed of my sinful nature, I continuously questioned why God would even want me to be in His company. Initially my inexperience hindered me from understanding that true forgiveness was dependent on genuine and sincere confession and repentance. Bitterness, anger, and animosity were my companions. God's nature is abounding in love and His desire is to forgive those who call upon Him (Psalm 86:5).

Once I understood and accepted God's nature, discovering the truth of God's word as it related to me, a woman and how that truth applied to my life in today's world became my single focus. The pursuit of revelation through God's word and its application began a wonderful transformation in my heart that would prepare and equip me for a journey in whatever God would have me do (2 Timothy 3:14-17). I consciously became aware of how thirsty and hungry I was for God's teachings. My appetite became insatiable. "Blessed are those who hunger and thirst for righteousness, for they shall be filled," (Matthew 5:6). To my realization, God was with me all the time, waiting patiently for me, watching over me. Yet in all my anger, pain and self-absorption I was unable to hear God calling me home. In the end, realization set in. I…as the prodigal daughter only needed to return home to be forgiven.

Holy Spirit

Incredibly once I decided to accept Jesus Christ as my Savior, a wonderful thing started to cultivate within the deepest recesses of my soul. It was a slow yet continuous process of awareness through the aid of the Holy Spirit which encouraged me and increased my belief in a chance for a new life. I had to recognize and understand that through Christ's blood I was redeemed (Ephesians 1:7). It was the Holy Spirit who enabled me to see my sinful nature, and let me be blunt…it was ugly!

Jesus, during his ministerial life on earth spoke to the people as a loving teacher, teaching us how to pray as the Sermon of the Mount illustrates. Forgiveness, as I came to realize, is an essential part of the healing process necessary for growth because all work by the Holy Spirit is completed internally. In retrospect if we forgive those who do us wrong, our Heavenly Father will forgive us (Matthew 6:12). The best medicine was to make certain my heart was pure and without fault before approaching my Heavenly Father in prayer. When I allowed the Holy Spirit to move within me, he released my spirit to grow in Christ through my dependency in Christ. It was through the working of the Holy Spirit within me that enabled me to begin to forgive myself. The freedom that is availed to us in order to draw near to God also allows God to draw near to us (James 4:8).

Guidance

Having to surrender the life I knew and depending on a Sovereign God was paralyzing. It was difficult and heartbreaking when it came to surrendering something I had held onto for a lifetime; control of every aspect of my life. Even with God's assertion I had to continuously keep my mind focused on God. Since change is inevitable, the uncertainty of change is uncomfortable for many people. Knowledge, experience, and routine in one's life fosters' security.

We marry and start our lives depending on one another. Then along comes one day, and you find yourself without the structure or support you worked so hard to build and you are left to face life and all of its responsibilities alone. I found myself in the predicament of raising my son single handedly. What could I do? Although family and friends are there to help support one through these trials, one becomes distraught and devastated. Yes, it is true they may help you in the beginning, but sometimes family and friends can (unknowingly) lead you in the wrong decisions that can lead to further destruction. I struggled for years with the fact that I believed divorce was my fault. Wondering why? What had I done? In reality, it wasn't me. I was alone and needed guidance. I had to accept that fact, and once I did I began asking for guidance from the Holy Spirit and believing in God's Son (John 3:16). Once I had freely given my life to become a true disciple, then I become His (1 Corinthians 6:19-20), and once I did, nothing could change that or separate me from God's love (Romans 8:38-39). When circumstances changed, I could always depend on God for strength, and guidance. Since God never changes (Hebrews 1:10–12), I was able to learn to trust a Sovereign and loving God in times of transition according to His purpose (Romans 8:28).

If I was to fully receive God's promise, I was required to continuously grow in my walk with the Lord Jesus Christ. In order to understand the nature of God's promises, I had to first understand the attributes of God. Jesus speaks about God's blessings and favor upon his people throughout the New Testament, in that if "We are children of God, then we are heirs – heirs of God and co-heirs with Christ," (Romans 8:17). Moreover, if I included the Old Testament as well, I was then able to grasp the overall picture of the blessings for an abundant life in Christ.

Let us consider the fact that there are many who upon receiving Christ, are afraid to move forward and continue to hold onto the only life they have ever known. The life that they are comfortable with, yet make them miserable. What kept me there was the "comfort zone" to which I was also accustomed too. Others may be so dependent on immorality, lust, drunkenness and wild parties that they are unwilling to attain freedom from those chains. Many are afraid of what their peers may think or say and many more have been deceived by the "god of this age who has blinded the minds of the unbelievers so that they cannot see the light of the gospel of the glory of Christ, who is the image of God," (2 Corinthians 4:4). I too was one of those individuals caught up and blinded by the world around me. Sucked into the pit of despair, loneliness, hatefulness, disparity, misery, sorrow, and tempted daily by dishonesty, corruption, deceitfulness and trickery.

Yet, the Parable of the Sower (Matthews 13) is an illustration of how Jesus' teachings drew from ordinary accounts of everyday life to convey his spiritual or moral truths. When the Lord issues a call to those who call themselves by His name, I had to leave my love for this world behind and find my hope, security, and satisfaction in God alone. Only then, would God fulfill his purpose for me.

It is with anticipation that I believed and held firm to the fact that Jesus promised us the Holy Spirit. If you feel lost, are having difficulties or just feel hopeless, you can always "Depend on the Lord; trust him, and he will take care of you," (Psalm 37:5). Did you know that before Jesus left his disciples, he promised to send them the Holy Spirit to guide them? Since God himself manifested the Holy Spirit, we can trust that it will also guide us in complete integrity (John 16:13).

Strength

When I choose to follow Christ, I, as a believer, knew I was in for difficulties and challenges. Asking for strength through prayer was and continues to be important in maintaining my strong walk. Although I recognized the fact that I had many weaknesses, I knew God was there to be my strength and was never far off if I called out to Him (Psalm 22:19).

What kept me from giving up the fight for truth? Where did I find the ability to hold onto my integrity when I felt weary and wanted to give up? I had to first build a foundation of courage. Weakness, worry, resentment, and anxiety were not going to be the catalyst to my failure. My past marriages were proof of that. How about decades of regret? Have you ever felt that way? Nevertheless, here was a loving, faithful God who was willing to accept me for what I was, a sinner and a failure; yet loved me unconditionally. Failing God was out of the question. I had to set in motion the wheels necessary to begin the process of transforming my old self into the new person by allowing the Hands of the Potter to mold me into his perfect plan. By allowing the Holy Spirit of God to live in me not only gave me strength, I also received wisdom and the assurance that I, a daughter of God, would receive the blessing of His glory upon finishing the fight. Those difficulties and storms I began to encounter I viewed as challenges. Challenges and hurdles which life was so determined to place in my life to throw me off my course of obedience in Christ Jesus.

As I had previously mentioned, Satan was not happy in losing another sinner, for while I was sinning, he had nothing to worry about. As soon as I had the smallest inkling of wanting plentitude, abundance and improved healthier relationships, he began to impress upon me how unworthy I was of that lifestyle. A lifestyle God has promised to me and/or anyone who accepts His Son, Jesus Christ, if I only held fast, stood firm and was not afraid (Exodus 14:13).

Every life has daily contact with change such as marriage, career, children, illness, relocations, divorce, and retirement. Some changes maybe voluntary, others may be forced by circumstances. Some changes may bring joy; other changes sorrow and confusion. If I believed God could make all changes positive; He would then strengthen the experiences for those under His authority. Since women respond to life's changes in different ways, it can be contributed to the fear about the unknown. In times of transition, women often lack self-confidence and others may experience frustration, depression, loneliness, and pain. I know I did. The only antidote for these feelings is faith and active obedience.

How great it is to know that when I have to face a trial, challenge or hurdle, God provides me with the strength I need to fight the good fight. Each time a new hurdle or challenge came my way, and knowing that I was still weak, I ran to the only thing I knew would save me…the waters of life…God's word. "You armed me with strength for battle; you made my adversaries bow at my feet," (Psalm 18:39).

As mentioned, there were numerous occasions when I was confronted with Satan's trickeries. However, when faced with difficulties, instinctively I trusted God's written word. God is faithful and will provide the means to stand up under it (1 Corinthians 10:13). He supplies the comfort I need - that no matter what I faced, God was, is, and will always be faithful. God loved us and through his grace he gave us a good hope and encouragement that continues forever," (2 Thessalonians 2:16). My Maker provides me with encouragement and strengthens me in everything I say and do. It does not mean that on occasions I will not trip, fall, or even stumble; I would not be human. Knowing God is always there to help me through those times assures me of his faithfulness. "If the Lord delights in a man's way he makes his steps firm, though he stumbles, he will not fall, for the Lord upholds him with his hand," (Psalm 37:23-24).

I was always one who when I had a need, my hope was that the Lord would meet and fulfill the need. James tells us that "You do not have because you do not ask," (James 4:2). We should never assume that God will automatically give it to us. Why, then was I so presumptuous in assuming I was any different? Humbling myself by slowly discarding my pride was one of the steps taken which enabled and provided an avenue to come before the Lord in earnest prayer with the belief and conviction that He would provide. "The effective fervent prayer of a righteous man avails much," (James 5:16).

The challenge to accept the reality of change is hard work and can be difficult. For that reason, encouragement should be provided by those who have experienced change. Difficulties will arise and when they do, it is important to study Scripture while facing a life change. Receiving inner strength from God during stressful times can result in God's richest blessings forever (2 Corinthians 4:7-18). Experiencing change might be a gift from God that may widen, deepen and heightened your personal relationship with the Lord. I have felt God's empowering strength with me in times of need. Changes in my life have caused me to remember that God is faithful yesterday, today, and forever (Hebrews 13:8).

63

Comfort

Comfort was non-existent during my relationships. My husbands were not the comforting types. The pain, resentment, and bitterness only grew during my marriages. Consequently, the strain of separation and divorce was clearly overwhelming and paved the way to receive the greatest comfort imaginable. Although I was married, I was alone within my marriages. The lack of responsibility and accountability by my husbands' only strengthened me while single-handedly raising Daniel. Being a single mom proved to be a wonderful joy. I can only believe that my son was God's gift to me in that, while I was unable to see what my future held, God did. The relationship that I built with my son Daniel was due to God's glorious intervention.

Daniel was my sidekick, we went everywhere together and over the years, the relationship continued to grow in closeness. In retrospect, I honestly believe it was my son Daniel, through God's faithful love, who kept me strong and grounded. Such comfort allowed me to focus on our future. What a great comfort to know that I was not alone in times of distress. Comfort comes from knowing that when I wait patiently on the Creator, He will always hear my cry (Psalm 40:1) for He knows me intimately and knows my needs even before my mind forms the thought (Matthew 6:8).

It was only with the dawning of the morning and the start of a brand new day that I was able to forget the loneliness of the night once confronted with the responsibility of work, school, or just life. I endeavored to stay active doing just about anything to keep my thoughts focused on positive matters and away from the emotional hurt which accompanied my nights. Walking through the various phases of hurt in an attempt to recover and heal, I asked God to provide me with a sign of His immense goodness, "For you O' Lord have helped me and comforted me," (Psalm 86:17).

I was incapable of understanding why I was destined to deal with that long painful and heartbreaking period in my life. When anything transpired, it was always I who asked "Why me Lord?" What have I ever done to you? Why would you do that to me? I know everyone has questioned God in some point in their lives. I was no different. Yet, through God's grace the Holy Spirit began to open my eyes by removing the scales once affixed. By increasing my understanding it slowly allowed me to recognize that the true focus was by no means...me. How self-centered I was. It has always been all about Him...Jesus Christ.

We are sometimes unable to conceive the fact that there is a God who leads us in the direction he wants us to travel in order for us to see His hand at work. I have always been an avid reader and it so happened that one day while I was reading Scripture, I came across several verses in Proverbs. God responded to me in such a subtle way so as to comfort me with His words. It is those words I run to when my mind begins to question my circumstances. "Trust in the Lord with all your heart and lean not on your own understanding, but in all your ways acknowledge Him and He will make your path straight," (Proverbs 3:5-6). It is this verse that reminds me that no matter what hurdles I was destined for, even if I did not understand Gods way, believing and trusting in Him provides a safety net in my life. Moreover, it was after I found this verse that I truly felt comforted. Many were the days that uncertainty reared its ugly head, and when it did, I was able to crush it as my Christian walk became stronger.

Have you ever been challenged? Say...in sports, school or even work? Were your thoughts of winning? How did it make you feel? Strong, invincible as you could accomplish anything? We all have that competitive will. I was presented with a challenge unbeknownst to me. It was this. The challenge was for me to become a warrior in God's army. Wow...what a challenge! All through school I was competitive and loved to win. It was an enormous challenge and one I hated to refuse to back out of. In fact, in order to make it more interesting, I accepted the challenge against myself.

During my youth I was taught to do well in school, and receive good grades if I was to advance in life. Once I became an adult, it was a process of continuously striving to advance myself in life by acquiring additional education, degrees, and certifications. I was one of those individuals whose accomplishment was to attain new heights; call me an advancing soul.

In reality, my curiosity to discern if in all honesty, it was possible to truly feel God's presence, love and comfort impelled me to accept the challenge. When striving towards a change which will improve the quality in one's life whether financially, socially or relational, it is paramount to search for an increase in knowledge. I began my quest within the pages of the Bible and found Scriptures, which filled me with comfort to continue my walk while contemplating the fact that if I looked for God I would be able to find Him, if my purpose and intentions were too genuinely seek Him (Jeremiah 29:13). Ok, that was a good start. I began to feel like a treasure hunter, always searching and seeking, never slowing down for fear of missing a clue.

It was through prayer, tears, sometime sobs, and personal conversation that one night, when I least expected it, the God of all creation, our Heavenly Father put his arms around me, held me and told me that He loved me. Whatever I was holding onto at that moment was lifted away and in its place was an overwhelming feeling of pure unadulterated joy and peace that could only come from our Lord and Savior Jesus Christ. What an incredible experience! I was hooked! If that was just a small illustration of what life was going to be like in the presence of and walking with God's Son, I would gladly choose Him. After that incredible experience, my senses had an epiphany and the leap manifested within me the understanding of how my life would no longer exist without the sustenance attained through a personal relationship with Jesus Christ. My life has never been the same. What an incredible journey!

Chapter Three

POWER OF FAITH

Developing faith was by no means an easy task. Faith does not come easy; especially to one whose conditioning is foreign to the way of Christian teachings. I was one of those. During my youth years, I was to some extent aware of the existence of a God. Growing up in New York, I was brought up in the Catholic faith and vaguely remember attending church. I believe I have mentioned in a previous chapter, how I have always felt a calling deep down in my soul during my youth. Unable to express those feelings and unaware of what I was truly feeling, my only recourse was to ask my parents if I could attend church. My parents did not attend service, yet on my persistence, they agreed to allow my sister and I to go in order to expand our intellect.

Of the few occasions I attended a Catholic church, there were not many which stood out in my mind as having any impact. My Catholic experience, even though short, did not fulfill my education requirements and left me lacking the knowledge I pursued. Emptiness remained in my heart and it was not until many years later that my faith would increase with my knowledge of an Omnipotent God. The moment the Holy Spirit started working within me, I began to grow in faith. For many years I prayed for deliverance and if my prayers were not answered, I lost faith. My impatience kept me from receiving the reward God had intended for me through His perfect timing. One might assume that if we are to receive what we have asked for, that unless one has extraordinary faith, it is

67

useless to pray for it. That is not so, the faith to simply pray is what is essential.

When my faith seemed dull, it was always best for me to search myself while asking the Holy Spirit to intervene and assist me in discovering what may be the underlying cause. I held onto my faith, remembering everything is done in God's perfect timing and should never assume God has not worked nor will He respond to my prayer.

Whether the underlying cause was unconfessed sin; the sin of disbelief; the sin of unforgiveness in my heart, or any other cause, I always take the time to resolve those issues with those I believe harmed me. Unforgiveness is physically damaging to the soul. Harboring ill will towards anyone can be destructive in my life and towards my prayers, as prayer will be ineffective until all hurt and resentment are resolved.

While writing this book, my faith was once again tested. My enemy the devil manipulated my employer to influence several owners' decision which led to my dismissal. My adrenalin immediately began coercing through my veins at the unwelcomed news; my mind flooding with thoughts of one such previous ordeal. Shaken at first, I was able to collect my thoughts after a few moments. There were two ways of reacting to the news when confronted with this reality. One form was destructive; the other was accepting the news as an opportunity for advancement. I chose the latter and began to secure my belongings. Dealing with such an ordeal previously provided the reinforcement and foundation I needed to encourage my faith and left me with the overall impression of peace. "God," I said. "You have always been in control. I have full faith in your ability to take care of and meet all my needs. Help me to understand and guide me in the direction of your Will."

Faith is the glue that keeps a bond between me and God. Faith believes in the manifestation of unseen things. If one truly wants to find God, one must have faith and the unwavering belief that He exists (Hebrews 11:6). Believing that God exists in the presence of adversity no matter how difficult or how desperate I felt during the long period of unemployment in 2002 and most recently (Psalm 119:58) is pleasing to Him. For that reason living faith is filling one's mind with God's word instead of letting one's mind become filled with challenges of the day. Faith is a result of one's desperate attempt to overcome difficult situations through the mighty power of prayer.

Believing

How incredibly arduous it was for me to believe in anyone, let alone an unseen Deity. Being able to believe in something or someone comes from one's ability to either assess credibility for one's self, the acceptance of authenticity based on verified information, or to have a conviction in an assurance. The inability to have personal communications within my marriages brought on a sense of distrust, distrust led to skepticism, and onto disbelief. In view of the fact that all three of my husbands were unfaithful, I had no other choice than to reconsider my position and start believing in myself to provide for the welfare of my son. Believing that I could depend on someone other than myself to support us was to defeat the purpose of survivorship. Self-sacrificing developed a passion within me for self-dependence. From that moment on I constructed a wall which kept me protected from my ability to believe in men. The wall became impenetrable.

In looking back, I am unable to pinpoint the exact date or hour in which my perception of believing altered from myself to God. If one is to accept the fact that one's perception can be altered, one has to first understand that faith is a nominal form of the verb "to believe." The Greek word for faith is "pistis, while "to believe" is pisteuein." Both words connote the idea of trust and confidence. Is not trust and confidence the basis for believing in family, friends, relationships? In order to protect myself from the pain, I had no other recourse than to build a solid perimeter wall around me. Year after year and brick by brick my wall was fortified by sufferance. The size and thickness of the wall I constructed was of no consequence for the Omnipotent God. How foolish was I in my self-absorption to ever think God would be incapable of breaking through my defenses. Since God has the ability to do whatever He wills it was through His goodness and righteousness which slowly began to purge each brick that encompassed my barrier of protection. God's sovereignty has created all and has determined everything that has happened and is to happen; and in doing so has caused man to believe his volition.

Believing goes hand in hand with faith. One is unable to do well without the other. How can one have faith if there is no belief that God is capable of all things? You will begin to notice a wonderful change that can only come from His grace and the power of the Holy Spirit (2 Corinthians 12:9). As the transformation began in me, it was easier for me to understand that God had a plan and purpose for my life (Psalm 138:8). I had to believe it, for anything less would have sabotaged my future. For God's requirements are simply put; He wants us to be available to all that he would do through us. God will never give up on me if I continue to believe that He will "Fulfill His purpose in my life," (Philippians 1:6) while concluding everything I entrust to Him (Philippians 2:13).

Hebrews 11:1 gives us the best definition of what faith is "Faith is being sure of what we hope for and certain of what we do not see." When understanding that God created everything from a formless substance, acceptance by His command of that, is what encourages me to continue to grow in my beliefs. The only obligatory and vital initial response of man to God's grace is faith. My current situation will build upon the faith I currently have. It provides the channel by which the Holy Spirit connects with my soul to aid in my belief. By further exploration into Hebrews 3:8, we can gather just how one relates rightly with God. "But my righteous one will live by faith." It is through the unshakable solid belief, confidence and the assurance that God is faithful and will prevail (Hebrews 10:23). Moreover, belief is my confidence in God's power that allows me to act on God's promises.

By recognizing the divine design in one's life, and esteems Christ above all, one can overcome tremendous odds. Although this conflict and difficulty attacked my life, believing and holding onto my faith allows me to identify and conquer those corruptive and impure thoughts or actions, which would impair my personal growth or intended service. Accepting the fact that we lack the means by which to control circumstances exemplifies the reality of how vulnerable we really are. If you believe in Jesus and receive Him as your Savior, your eternal destiny has been confirmed. "If you believe, you will receive whatever you ask for in prayer," (Matthew 21:22). Never give up believing there is a Sovereign God who will deliver us in time of need. Believing - is a bridge between the gap we have with God, which allows us to get closer. Jesus got it right, when he said anything is possible if a person believes.

Trusting

Upon accepting Christ, the first requirement necessary was to repent of my sins. This did not denote a partial one hundred and eighty degree turn; on the contrary, it required a complete three hundred and sixty degree turnaround. Altering my ways and turning from sin allowed me to wholeheartedly turn to faith. Early on I ascertained that without true repentance trusting was fruitless, empty and superficial. By striving to live a Christian life without total dependency on God resulted in emotional distress, heartache and disappointments. This was indicative of my inability and lack of will power to make the choice to either continue the gratification of my own desires or choose freedom from slavery. Weighing the choices was not difficult, I chose the latter.

Trusting was difficult at first as my failed relationships can attest to. Here was God who loved me unconditionally, yet in spite of that and before I could reciprocate, I found myself broken and to the point of

71

almost homelessness before I seized God's hand. As the hands of time continued to move forward my trust in God grew stronger. With that, I committed myself to envision the outcome of my relationship with God, no matter the opposition. It was a journey which proved to be similar to an "e" ticket ride at Disneyland. The more determined I was towards prayer and studies, the more my life began to gravitate towards a positive outcome. My old desires were slowly dissipating while new thoughts and dreams were forming and taking their place. I was meeting new people who were Christians and whom God specifically chose to assist me during those specific periods in my life.

Individuals come into one's life for a season and even for a lifetime. Those individuals who enter our lives are there for a specific purpose and since we are unsure of how long those individuals will be in our lives, one should cherish and appreciate the time given in service. I have been blessed by many of God's servants who have drawn near to my existence from all walks of life.

While I tried to catch a glimpse of what the future held by trying to will it; God is the only Being capable of such a realization – He is Omniscient. Recognizing the significance while remembering God is in control of the end results, I could now identify with what was happening in my life. He was directing individuals into my life to emotionally support, guide and assist in my future growth while I developed a larger dependency on Him and through that dependency I received the friendship of such a girlfriend. Her name was Missy. Our friendship matured and developed throughout a twenty year span. Her unconditional love and support facilitated the opportunity for healing and growth. Friendships are such a gift despite the length of the season. My friendship lasted for an extended season; nevertheless one day it ended. Albeit, I was unsure of why friendships end, my stance was one of extreme gratefulness for her presence in my life. God in His unending wisdom blesses us with various seasons. It is a measure of love that is given to us by His grace. "Every good and perfect gift is from above coming down from the Father," (James 1:17).

Power of Faith

I recall one incident wherein Missy, my wonderful friend came to my rescue. It so happened that on one afternoon while I was busily cleaning the house, Edwardo came up to me and informed me that he intended to work late. "Don't worry, about giving me a ride, I have already made plans with Pete, your brother-in-law to give me a ride home," he said. "You won't be too late, will you?" I replied. "No, I should be home around nine o'clock." "Ok," I responded and continued cleaning the house. As evening approached my apprehension increased. By eleven o'clock my anxiety escalated into sheer fear. Immediately I picked up the receiver and dialed my sister. "Hello," she said. "Hi is Pete home yet?" I asked. "Oh yes, Pete arrived hours ago." "Really," I responded. "Do you know if Edwardo made plans for Pete to drop him home after work?" She replied "None that I know of, but just a moment. Let me ask Pete." Muffling the phone piece, she questioned Pete. Speaking into the mouth piece once again she replied "Pete said he hasn't spoken to Edwardo at all today." "Really...thanks," I said and hung up the phone. Perplexed, I turned my attention to the clock, it glowed eleven thirty p.m.

Missy lived a couple of buildings down from my apartment within the same complex. Knowing Missy kept late night hours, I lifted the receiver and started dialing. She answered after the first ring. "Hello?" "Hey it's me," and began to explain in detail what was going on. She agreed to accompany me at that late hour down to Pete's office building. Desperate, my adrenalin was peaking. Still dressed in our pajamas, we got into my car, punching the gas once the car hit the on ramp. There we were two wild women streaking down the Antelope Valley Freeway (I14) from Palmdale to the San Fernando Valley at midnight. My intention was to catch Edwardo red-handed in a lie. A forty-five minute drive to the Valley was completed in the span of half an hour, arriving at the designated location. Parking the vehicle at the rear of the building, we got out and started to walk. The parking lot was empty except for a couple of vehicles. Spanning the area I veered right and noticed a station wagon belonging to Edwardo's co-worker Genna drive past us. I screamed "There they are!" and we rushed back to my car. Jumping inside, I gunned the engine, tires screeching, I shifted the engine into first gear and the car shot forward like a bat out of hell. Driving as fast as I possibly could in hopes of catching up to them. In the end it became hopeless; I had lost them. How infuriated I was! When I arrived home Edwardo was in bed pretending to be asleep.

God intervened. Once again my emotions were clouding my judgment. If not for my guardian Angel Missy, chosen to be by my side during this event, in all probability my life would have taken another direction. I would have killed them both.

God's infinite wisdom places people to assist and carry one through disappointments and heartbreaks. I called upon someone who I trusted explicitly to watch out for my interests, and that someone was Missy. Recalling that event to mind, made it less effortless to trust in God once my decision was made to trust in Him for nothing less than all. Trusting in the Most High by believing in His son Jesus Christ, who died for me and was resurrected, provided the avenue to have a life pleasing to God.

Obedience

We are taught obedience at an early age. Our parents teach us to be obedient to the laws which are placed within one's home. These laws have been handed down from generation to generation and are culturally different by family. Laws teach us, protect us and prepare us to become acclimated to new future social environments. We are taught at a very young age to respect the laws handed down to us by our parents and grandparents. As we mature, we learn that every aspect of society has its governing body of laws we must also comply with. The educational system also has regulations which must be observed. Being disobedient at school usually meant a visit to the Principal's office; consequently punishment would be issued. In today's society, punishment is dispensed based on the offense. Before arriving at driving age, we are required to study the motor vehicle laws through classes and driving lessons before a license to drive can be attained. As we travel through life, acceptance of the governing laws is a part of our lives. One must adhere to them to work well in society.

My family was by no means dysfunctional; in fact my teenage years were pretty good. I maintained a grade point average of 3.9, had good friends and worked an eight hour shift while attending school. At the ripe old age of seventeen, I…in my infinite wisdom decided to run away from home. I wanted to see the world and explore new territories. Determined to be a free woman, I packed my bags and after everyone was asleep, I quietly headed towards the door of the apartment. I stopped by the kitchen table to leave a note assuring my folks I would be alright. I picked up the bags and headed towards the front door. My hand reached for the door handle. Twisting it opened, I slowly pulled the door inward so as not to make the hinges squeak loudly. I stopped at the doorway to take a final look; the familiar surroundings of the only life I knew. I inhaled deeply and released my breath, closing the door behind me.

Was I mindful of my parents? No. Did I consider their feelings, no…not in the least. My disobedience brought them feelings of disappointment, pain, hurt, self-doubt in their parenting abilities, and much, much more. My self-indulgence became the driving force by which my decisions were rooted. A friend convinced me to rent a room in her apartment in Pasadena. In reality, I did not foresee any problems. My focus was on only one person…me. Contemplating the overall picture prior to making a decision would have prevented my parents from the agony they faced the following morning.

My decision to move into the apartment opened an avenue in which to experiment with drugs. Primarily marijuana was the choice, then I moved onto Tai a brand of weed. Angel Dust was next on the list of "should try." Next on the agenda was Cocaine with a final stop at Speed. After a little over a month into my great adventure realm of the big world, reality set in. My 1974 Ford Maverick, puke green in color, began to slowly break down. The breakdown of my car instigated the ensuing events.

Unable to financially meet the required car repair expenditure, my choices were slim. Either travel from Pasadena to North Hollywood through public transportation to my current employment or solicit a ride from a friend. The single option readily available was to take public transportation. After several attempts of trying to endure the harsh actuality of public transportation along with the nightly drug usage, prevented me from performing my vocational responsibilities. I received a call from my employer terminating my employment. Alone and broke this prodigal daughter, contacted her Dad to help restore her self-worth by asking for forgiveness prior to returning home. My parents welcomed me with open arms. How much more will God welcome home his prodigal children?

God the Creator of the universe handed down the laws to Moses. God as our Heavenly Father has given His children those laws, which are a blueprint of how one is to conduct oneself and dwell by. Obedience to those laws help guide, direct and uphold us with its truth. John tells us that Christ loved us first and because of it, our obedience to His commandments begins through our love for Christ (1John 4:9 & 19). The key here is love. When you love someone, you respect them. When you respect them, you obey them. Once I fell in love with Christ, my love was transformed into the basis for my obedience. In reality, my perspective altered and I began to see the world through totally different eyes, the eyes of Christ. Placing my faith in the Lord provided a conduit directly to obedience. Accepting Christ into my life was the best decision I had ever made. Not only did He transform me into a new person, the transformation originated deep within my soul. The word of God says that we are to respect and honor our parents. The laws that God gave us constitute the basis of the moral principals currently followed today.

Following the commands of the Holy Father will deliver one from the oppression currently accosting one. Disobey and Satan will continue his control over one's life. Obedience to the law brings blessings of the Lord upon the individual who preservers in their commitment to Christ. My faith is reflected in my obedience in my daily life. Once I experienced deliverance in my life, I could no longer revert to disobedience. Following the commands God outlined, was for me - essential. At first adhering to the new way of thinking was foreign and unfamiliar, yet gradually I began to accustom myself and as time went on those teachings became part of my daily routine.

An illustration of how the Lord freely offers everything necessary to give His people life can be found in John 10:10. Obedience assures us of an abundant life. Throughout the Bible, we find passages that command us to obey the Lord (Deuteronomy 4:30, 11:1-31, Deuteronomy 7:27, Acts 5:29). The blessings of God are not specific to any one area of life; but encompass' every aspect. How wonderful to know that God can overall bless us in everything. My obedience flows out of my love for God. Acts of obedience reflects our desire to please and love the Lord.

When I became a servant of the Lord, I saw life in a whole new perspective. I began to embrace God's teachings and those teachings allow me to expand my territory as I moved into a different way of living life. "Because of the service by which you have proved yourselves, men will praise God for the obedience that accompanies your confession of the gospel of Christ and for your generosity in sharing with them and with everyone else," (2 Corinthians 9:13). Obedience to the Lord results in a life of abundance, prosperity, and joy, but only when we listen and obey. My choice not to obey my parents brought upon me pain, unemployment and disgrace.

The Lord offers all that brings overwhelming satisfaction and gathers to Himself all who respond to Him in faith and obedience. If we respond to God in obedience, we would then enjoy the good life. Obedience is a life-long endeavor.

Hope

Hope is distilled in us through the very essence of Christ. Walking in hope frees us from being fearful of what is to come. Rejoicing in the knowledge that our God will come to save us from our oppression magnifies our love for Him.

Late one night in 1982, I was sitting on my living room sofa sobbing. Edwardo and I had another fight. He had just gone to bed and was immediately able to fall asleep as substantiated by the loud snoring emanating from the bedroom. I…on the other hand was wide awake, crying and hoping beyond hope, I would be able to find peace within my marriage. My eyes blinded by tears, I changed the channel. As I was surfing through the stations I came across TBN – the Trinity Broadcast Network. On the screen was Ephraim Zimbalist, Jr., an old television actor from my childhood days. I lifted my hands to my face trying to wipe away the tears clouding my vision. He was sitting comfortably in a warn leather chair reading Scripture from the Bible. As I watched him, my mind raced back to a happier former time recalling the series. Listening to his soothing voice, calmed me.

Leaving the television on I walked into the kitchen; there were dishes that needed to be washed. Standing in front of the sink, I turned on the water; my thoughts trying to formulate the significance of why my marriage was not functioning. My conscious mind was in turmoil. Conversing with God I asked "Is this was all I am destined for?" It was nothing more than a rhetorical question. By no means was I expecting a response. I drew my mind back from my thoughts to concentrate on the task at hand. In the middle of washing a glass my eyes began to fill with tears once again. Lowering my eyes I noticed my hands in soapy water. Immediately a sense of hopelessness overwhelmed me. Crying out in desperation I yelled "God…please help me!" My words were not fully uttered when instantly I felt an overpowering and incredible rush filling every inch of my being with God's peace, joy, love, and hope. God's Holy Spirit was upon me sweeping away the despondency, desperation, pain and hopelessness oppressing me and filled me with a sense of new found hope of a better tomorrow. In gratitude I fell to my knees. What an incredible experience!

Any delay in fulfillment can sometimes cause disappointments, which can cause depression within one's body and spirit. Awareness of hope produces encouragement and gives vitality to the body and spirit. Hope is the realization that God wants more for us. Placing our hope in God provides a safe and joyful way to walk through the highway of life and rejoice greatly when we receive the everlasting gladness and joy from Him. Hope is the blessed assurance of our future destination while strengthening the weak and fearful. God's love is revealed to us by the Holy Spirit. Christ died for us sinners and it is in that gift that we place our hopes. We should encourage ourselves and strengthen our hearts with the hope of Christ's coming (James 5:7-11) focusing on that hope produces patience under oppression.

Hope is magnificent as it allows one to see a better future for our children, family and friends. When I encounter situations of suffering, it is in those times that God molds me and shapes my life. It is also in those times that God shapes my character through perseverance, while the end result is hope. This sustenance gives the Holy Spirit time to help us during those seasons.

In Romans 8:31-39 Paul encourages us by announcing that God is for us. He will freely give us all things, He has justified us, and He prays for us. The Holiness of God symbolizes the true nature of God's attributes. He grants us the courage and hope to guide us along each day. He is the way through rough and trying times, and although we cannot see, and are unsure of everything, if we search His promises, we can then understand that it is hope which lifts our faltering courage and renews our spirits.

When I began reading the Bible more thoroughly, the screen in my mind began to grasp instantaneously, the attributes of God. These attributes were revealed and made evident by the precious promises by God to His children. There are numerous diverse promises scattered throughout the Bible, in spite of that, they are God's promise and God's Word can be trusted.

As I have touched on previously, the fulfillment of God's promises are relative to our obedience to God (Deuteronomy 11:27). In reflecting on the job I previously mentioned, it was hope which I maintained and held steadfast to that delivered me from the hands of the unethical employer. God is faithful because God is God, "The Holy one" (Hosea 11:9). When we "Hold unswervingly to the hope we profess" we can hold to the truth that God "Who promises is faithful," (Hebrews 10:23). For the Lord watches those who fear him and who's hope is in his unfailing love (Psalm 33:18).

Placing my hope in the Lord allows Him to renew my strength. I am then capable of soaring like eagles, I can run and not grow weary, and I can walk and not faint (Isaiah 40:3). It is amazing to read the words written down so many centuries ago, which to this day provides us with the Scriptures necessary to teach us to endure, while encouraging us and offering hope (Romans 15:4).

Peace

Our lives are daily littered with headlines that disturb our peace of mind. The pressure of work, family, friends, finances are all playing havoc within us. No matter what one tries to do, it is sometimes impossible to find the time to regroup. The turmoil I felt before becoming a believer was no less than an incredible self-worthlessness. No matter how hard I tried to make things right, I was unable to. Throughout my marriages there were many hours of dark tribulation in which I felt more and more dissatisfied and felt less and less secure.

During the period of unemployment in 2002, I became more anxious as the days past and as my future became unsure. Facing financial difficulties began to crush my spirit and I was unable to find peace in any hour of my day. The only hope that was readily available to me was the Bible. Walking around my apartment, sometimes in a daze, I thought "I know I have a copy of the Bible. Where is it? If I could just find a little peace, I know I could somehow make it through another day."

In reminiscing - I occasionally opened the Bible as a child and although I was unable to comprehend it (old KJV), I do recall, even at such a young age, how peaceful and reassured I felt when trying to understand it. It appears even then, something was pulling at my heart. I found my son's first Bible and began to read, shifting through the pages, first Psalms and then Proverbs. Peace can only be bestowed by God and striving for peace is effortless without God. Peace represents the absence of turmoil. It is a life that professes harmony and a right relationship with God. Inner spiritual peace can be achieved only if one walks in the Spirit regardless of strife.

In my twenty years of marriage and three husbands, peace was never regarded as anything achievable. Peace was short lived as difficulties always arose. When my days become pressure-packed with not enough hours in a day, I could now stop and take a moment to reflect and mediate on God's word. A few moments a day to meditate alleviated the pressures of stress and provided the relief necessary to continue through the day. The true peace of God protects ones heart and mind from worry, fear, and anxiety. "Do not be anxious about anything, but in everything, by prayer and petition, with thanksgiving, present your requests to God. And the peace of God which transcends all understanding will guard your heart and mind in Christ Jesus," (Philippians 4:6-7). These are words of assurance which profess a promise onto my being of tranquility, harmony, and freedom from strife. Although we were made in God's image, we are

81

incapable of understanding Gods plans in our lives. All one has to do is maintain the steadfast knowledge that we are never alone (Jeremiah 29:11). We have been given a guarantee that right in the mist of chaos, God will provide us with peace of mind.

It is through God's grace we gain self-control. Meditating on God's words can restore the peace to our soul (Isaiah 57:19). Enjoyment of an abundance of peace can be obtained if we attain a complete contempt of self (Psalm 119:165). God's presence in our lives allows Him to produce in us a quiet faith, hope and trust regardless of our daily surroundings or circumstances.

My career in property management spans over thirty years. The job has always been stressful and requires dedication, yet it has always been my passion. Managing retail or commercial properties necessitate a personality to withstand the demands placed upon ones persona. More often than not, long hours, an aptitude to make split second decisions and a spin doctoring attitude is undoubtedly required. That propensity promotes self-confidence and awareness in one's ability as a leader, which adds additional credence to an awareness and appreciation of how I want my life to interact with my peers and subordinates. Respect should be given and accepted. Anything less would jeopardize one's ability as a leader and team player. My vocation is stressful enough, however, when an outside obstacle enters into the equation, it not only makes working difficult, but unpleasant.

My recent encounter with my former employer promoted the necessity to maintain a Christian attitude no matter how difficult and disrespectful my employer became. His persona was enveloped in a negative aura surrounding his very essence which permeated the office the moment he entered. My days were filled with tension and uncertainty, while my nights were consumed struggling to recuperate from the strife and discord of the day. My daily ritual of worrying about tomorrow made it impossible to find peace. Then one night while diving through Scripture, I came across a specific verse. The verse read "Therefore do not worry

82

about tomorrow, for tomorrow will worry about itself. Each day has enough trouble of its own," (Matthew 6:34). I pondered that verse over and over again. Clarity ensued. Focusing on tomorrow before tomorrow arrived, meant I was attempting to meet God half way into tomorrow before God had a chance to prepare the means for my deliverance. Tomorrow is not written until the choices of today are finalized. Realizing the significance of the verse allowed my soul to obtain the peace it desperately seeked. During my quest for peace I asked God to help me to understand what it was He wanted me to learn from this situation. He responded with three simple words - "Pray for him." Immediately I felt my old self raising up again. Suppressing those unwelcomed emotions, I humbly adhered. Jesus invites us to "Love your enemies and pray for those who persecute you" (Matthew 5:44). Simply because I took those words to heart, peace manifested within my current situation.

Chapter Four

POWER OF PATIENCE

They say patience is a virtue; nevertheless it is a critical step when walking with Christ. The world is constantly moving and changing, despite of that, God always remains the same. In an attempt to keep up with the world, we haphazardly forget to wait on the Lord. Our world usually dictates how fast we move and what our day will entail. One believes that if we rush to meet God half way, the sooner one's trials will be over. Not so. God is a God of law, order and method. Society in its ever changing form programs us to change with it.

My vocation required that I attend weekly meetings. There were many times during those meetings wherein I was subjected to verbal degrading, belittling and disrespect all because of one individual's desperate need to satisfy his insatiable egotistical persona. Many times I asked myself why I was leaving myself open to this individual's abuse; while a battle raged within me as I weighed my situation. On one hand I loved everything about my job and on the other I was miserable. Working in this type of environment, promotes a sense of ineptitude, insecurity and anxiety. I pushed myself every morning to maintain a positive attitude. Recognizing I had an enemy within the ranks of upper management gave me the advantage and the opportunity to grow further in my walk. Familiarizing myself with my opponent's intricacies prepared me for daily battle. Every morning before leaving my home, I would put on the Armor of God (Ephesians 6:10-19). Always remembering that I was working for the Lord and whatever actions I performed while in my daily vocation, I was obligated to do it to the best of my ability (Colossians 3:22-24). Recognizing my need to work through this trial provided an avenue in which patience became the essential foundation to endure the hardship (James 5:8).

Requesting several measures of patience daily for almost a year should have made me walk away from my commitment to my employer, nevertheless I continued to tolerate my circumstances while faithfully and graciously waiting upon the Lord for deliverance. I chose to suffer the hardship and maintain dignity within my circumstance in order to participate in the joy when God revealed His glory (1 Peter 4:13).

Patience is one of the fruits of the Spirit that we learn about as we mature in our walk. Perseverance is the term to describe how faithfully one remains steadfast during time of attack and discouragement. Patience is the ability that one is given to endure trials without complaining and with calmness (James 1:2-4). There were many times when I asked God to allocate a larger measure of patience upon me. Much to my dismay, He did not. What God did present me with were many opportunities for patience. It was one more lesson tenderly dispensed for my edification.

We are to be persistent in accomplishing goods for a life time of commitment (2 Peter 1:5-7). We are to persevere in prayer (Ephesians 6:18), and in faith (Hebrews 12:1-2). When we are faced with hardships, we should patiently endure suffering for in the mist of suffering, God's strength is available for God's purpose to be carried out. A measure of patience can facilitate the means in which God provides one with the resources necessary to overcome great pain and suffering.

Let Go & Let God

Let go and let God - how difficult that sounds to all who are still in darkness and unable to see the light, or even for those who have eyes yet are blinded by ignorance. Letting go and letting God was the most difficult part of my walk. The Bible instructs us to listen to God rather than to focus on our own helplessness (Isaiah 51:1-23). When all one has to rely on is oneself, emancipating control of one's life produces gut wrenching trepidation and fear. The fear is what causes us to remain in our oppressive state. Fear is not our friend, it is our enemy. If one moves beyond the boundary of fear, one can gain knowledge of God's abundance for one's life. Fear is not in any way associated with the attributes of God (Romans 8:15). Fear is one of the numerous weapons used by Satan to maintain control over one's life. Breaking through the gut wrenching fear made it possible and provided an opportunity for me to let go and let God.

Moving beyond those prearranged boundaries provided the freedom to move towards developing a relationship with the Omniscient (All Knowing) God. I recall several occasions wherein my humanistic earthly desire sought to recant control from God and endeavored to execute the task myself. People tend to be selfish with time and if things do not seem to be progressing fast enough, we retract it and our impatience tends to distort our way of thinking; by allowing one to assume that one is capable of doing a better job and in less time than God can.

When we let go and let God, one steps out in faith or out of our known comfort zone. Letting go and letting God is thinking outside the box and outside the box is where we find God and our Lord Jesus Christ. Whenever I find myself in a situation that calls for me to step outside my known comfort zone, my thoughts have a tendency to revert back to Peter the Disciple. Peter along with the other disciples were crossing the Sea of Galilee in a small boat when suddenly the winds picked up. The waves began to assault their small boat. As the disciples were battling the wind, they looked out and saw Jesus walking on the water. Although scared, Peter's deep faith in Jesus was undoubtedly the instrument and the means by which Peter stepped out of his comfort zone and walked on water towards the Lord. Faith is the intermediary by which all things move towards and draws us closer to our Lord. However, it was not until Peter's attention and focus was diverted from Jesus that he began to sink (Matthew 14:28-31).

On many occasions I felt just as Peter did; scared, frightened and sinking into the deep recess of the waters. My faith faltered when facing circumstances greater than my ability to manage and control it. Yet, this story reminds me to continuously focus on what is truly the fundamental principal of our Lord, and never lose sight of the importance of having faith in God. Thus allowing Him to position and set in motion whatever plans He has for me.

We all know that the universe has order, if it did not we would not exist. This order could only have come to pass by and through divine intervention – an all encompassing God. Consequently, His plans for us require a period of germination as in any seed growth by hanging on to patience, hope and the unfailing belief that God will prevail.

As in anything that grows, time and love are what are necessary. Albeit, we are unable to see the entire picture of our life, God is able to. At times, we doubt that He is even present in our life. There is only one thing we have to remember and that is to recognize God is working silently in other people's lives in order to make His plan for you and me a reality. God will provide the necessary people, things or supplies in order for God's purpose to be carried out. The hardest part is waiting on the Lord; especially due to our current life style. God does everything in His perfect timing. He is never late or early. Society has become impatient through the modern technologies of today.

If we let go and let God, we are released from worrying about everything and can then work on one day at a time without having to ever borrow sorrow (Matthew 6:34). We can live and give it our best. For if we meet tomorrow's troubles before they are ours, it will only give rise to doubt and the healing powers of our Almighty God. When one is troubled, upset and sick at heart, it is best to remember God is ready and willing to share those burdens we find too heavy to bear. Letting go and letting God leads the way into a much happier and brighter day.

Spiritual Discipline – Growing in Christ

As with any training spiritual nourishment was necessary if I was to grow and develop in my spiritual maturity. Even though it was difficult for me at first to actually spend time reading the Bible, it was the only way to set in motion the spiritual process. The process begins with obedience to the Almighty and the faith resulting from my walk at the onset of my growth. Discipline was essential and a continual process which allowed me to mature and know God's will. Ultimate change in my attitude and commitment including personal training in prayer, worship, fellowship, bible study and service was mandated.

Breaking free from my street wise, controlling, independent and drug partying old self took an amazing effort on my part to achieve the goal I set for myself long ago. I am daily growing and spiritually developing. Undertaking such a large commission was - I knew to be a lifelong commitment. It is a committed process one should consciously pursue through the means of spiritual fellowship. Without spiritual discipline, one would be unable to walk with Christ or even grow and mature in one's faith (Hebrews 6:11-12). Spending time in the word began to stir wonderful and hopeful feelings within my soul. I was experiencing the renewal of my spirit.

For that reason it is crucial to remind ourselves that our minds are bombarded daily with negative sensations via the news, radio or visual Medias. My mind receives invading thoughts every second of my life, therefore mentally training myself to capture the negative thoughts that permeated my brain waves, allowed me to place into action a life time practice of controlling and accepting only positive thoughts. This is a routine I practice daily. Not an easy task, however, the ability to change your life is within you as it was with me. Discipline allows one to be delivered from sin and maintain one's relationship with Christ. Exclusive of spiritual discipline one is unable to receive the blessings of God's promises for those who practice diligently spiritual discipline. The Holy

Spirit is always working in my life and it aids me to grow in my relationship with God. Growing can be a struggle. Yet, as I matured spiritually I discovered inner strength that resulted in faithfulness, self-control and gentleness. Maturing requires the removal of all hindrances while seeking nourishment eagerly and with a pure heart. God's desire is only for our well being.

As incredible as it sounds, God provided for every one of my needs through my personal relationship with Him in prayer. His source is unlimited. When I truly seek God I can then renounce my problems and place them in God's hands. Simply believing that my needs will be met, continuously seeking Him, asking Him to fellowship with me during my daily travels in my ordinary road of life, and by thanking Him for being the loving God who controls every circumstance in my life. God's desire is for us to focus and grow in our ability to see Him in every significant and minuet circumstance as we begin to depend on Him solely.

I have been called to participate in God's mission to serve those less fortunate. Responding to His call is not only a privilege, it allows immediate access to God through His son Jesus Christ and in doing so provides the means and opportunity to personally witness to others. As I continue my studies and grow in my spiritual discipline, I am able to hold true that my Lord is my Shepherd. Following His call where ever He may lead assures me of His guidance and guarding as I travel through dark valleys.

Wisdom

Wisdom comes from the knowledge we gain from an event, encounter or experiences during one's lifetime. As a young girl, I was inexperienced to make any appropriate decision when situations arose. My young mind only wanted to spend the days playing outside with the other kids. I can still hear my mother's voice saying "Come straight home after school." Did I listen to my mother's advice? No. Not on this particular occasion. At the tender age of seven, I had no experience, knowledge or ability to understand the demands or the defenses required to protect myself from the outside world. One afternoon my selfishness got the better of me and with no regard for my mother's warning decided to stay in the playground after school. I was thoroughly enjoying the afternoon weather, swinging on the monkey bars with a classmate when I looked out across the playground and saw my mother crossing the street. "Oh…oh, I'm in for it now," I thought. I managed to climb down off the monkey bars at the same moment she grabbed my arm. "How did she get here so quick," I thought. Mom spanked me right in the middle of the playground and said, "What is wrong with you, young lady! I told you to go straight home… didn't I? Get moving!"

Walking home I instinctly knew the spanking I received was not the full punishment. When we arrived home, she told me to stand in the corner. "I'll be right back, don't you move," Mom said as she walked towards the kitchen. Collecting some rice from the container, she returned to the living room. Placing the rice on the floor, she said "Kneel on the rice and don't you move until I say you can. Do you understand me, young lady?" Crying, I mustered out a low "Yes," as I knelt down on the rice. Mom sat in the living room waiting for me to make any kind of move. Being such a small child an hour seemed like an eternity. "Why didn't I listen to Mom, I would have saved myself some grief," I thought.

Mom's instinct was to watch out for my welfare and ensure my development through dependency. As a child, mistakes happen naturally. Growing and developing into the woman I am today was based on the choices I made. Experiencing the peaks and the valleys throughout my life was indisputably a journey which granted access into acquiring knowledge and wisdom.

God also wants us to go to Him with every aspect of our life. Wisdom is received only when it is given by our mighty God. If we ask

Him, He will direct and give us more grace. Wisdom is given freely and abundantly to those who ask, seek and knock (Matthew 7:7-8; Luke 11:9-10). God wants to bless us with peace, joy and wisdom so that we can discern and be able to deal with one day at a time. Whenever I find myself being attacked with the day's issues reminding myself to stop and focus on God promotes wisdom. Refocusing on the one and only Jesus Christ can and does provide me with a safe haven from the attacks. When I humble myself, God's grace covers and lifts me. Our life is shaped by our thoughts. When we ask for wisdom, we obtain understanding. Wisdom is essential as it protects and watches over everything we do (Proverbs 4:5-6).

Wisdom is the divinely created system of laws that were positioned to protect the moral fibers of the universe. It is the basis of good sense and practical judgment. One should seek God's will and ask for God's wisdom when facing a major life decision. Prayerfully seeking God's perfect wisdom also goes hand in hand with knowing and committing to God's word.

A wise person is one who repeatedly acknowledges, relies and trusts in God's divine understanding. Fear of the Lord is the foundation of wisdom (Proverbs 1:7). For God's law provides the essential wisdom needed to obtain a life pleasing to God (Deuteronomy 29:14-19). An individual's mind that is open to the truth of God has the "Fear" attitude and is the attitude one must take for reverent obedience (Psalm 19:7 & 9). We can obtain wisdom by our own means, however, our wisdom is finite compared to the immeasurable wisdom and power of God (Deuteronomy 10:12). Fear is not indicative of sheer terror, but of respectful obedience of His laws. God gives me understanding while teaching me to be kind, so that I may judge all people with my heart and not my mind. In order for me to acquire wisdom, I must be faithful and in obedient service, for a true believer can revert once again to a lost condition.

Solomon was a great King of Israel as well as King David's son. One night Solomon had a dream. In the dream God spoke to Solomon and directed Solomon to ask God for whatever he wanted (1 Kings 3:5). Solomon loved the God of his father David and Israel wholeheartedly. So when Solomon responded to God's request it was not for power, long life, riches, or even the death of his enemies. He asked God to bestow upon him the gift of discernment. God was so pleased with Solomon's response God granted Solomon's request and not only did the Lord give Solomon a discerning and wise heart, but He blessed Solomon with everything he did not ask for! Solomon's proverbs were provided to enlighten the populace with wisdom, discipline, insights and guidance. Realizing that wisdom predestines knowledge, gives one an ample highway in which God can direct one uninterrupted road to life.

Building a Relationship with God

So often we try to have a relationship with others without truly getting to know them. We see through them, yet we never stop to really take them in. This is owing to the fact that we are so busy trying to impress them and win them over. I can honestly say my last relationship started out that way. Paul was obviously trying to impress me and I was so taken by his attention and charm, I did not even consider building a quality relationship based on a foundation of long term friendship. Our relationship was moving so fast at the onset, that it only led to our inability of perceptively knowing our compatibilities. Our self-centeredness was towards our physical needs. This left me feeling hollow and empty. The shallowness of our relationship only exposed our emotions to injury. Since Paul was not comfortable with commitment, when I called upon him for assistance, he was always unavailable. Consequently our relationship began to falter as his lack of accountability and responsibility grew.

When building a relationship with your fellow brother or sister, it is important to take the time to know him/her intimately. Personal questions are asked in order to ensure the individual is the one wanted in one's life. We become involved by nurturing, willingness to take the time and meditating on their words. Subsequently, it would provide us with the needed insight to make the correct decision as to their spiritual, mental, emotional, physical and social development. Once those attributes have been gathered then and only then can a determination be made on whether to move forward with the relationship.

In order for one to go directly to the Father, one must first begin to build a relationship with His son Jesus Christ. There is a new age belief that one can get to heaven by circumventing the acceptance and acknowledgment of Jesus Christ. This is not plausible as Scripture specifically tells us so (John 14:6). Accepting Jesus Christ as our Savior provides the means by which we receive everything necessary for us to grow in our walk with God. "You will seek me and find me, when you seek me with all your heart," (Jeremiah 29:13). I searched all my life for a relationship in which I would be loved and treated with respect. I, however, was not fortunate to find such an affiliation. In that respect, I set my sights on building a relationship with my Lord Jesus Christ and avail myself to the freedom Jesus had given me in going before the Father.

The world was not created by the big bang as scientists have us believing. The events of the universe were called into order by a compassionate gracious, long-suffering and faithful God (Isaiah 41:10), and a God with whom our relationship becomes a relationship with honesty, truth, and higher morals. It also allows one to begin to mature. Maturity permits our personality to change to one of peace, confidence and faithfulness.

As I grew in my intimate and personal relationship with God, God's word taught me to become good, kind and loving to all those I came in contact with. "I have loved you with an everlasting love; I have drawn you with loving kindness," (Jeremiah 31:3). Therefore, since everything is ordered by God, I had to become more dependent on God and less dependent upon man's approval in all aspects of my life. True happiness, earthly blessings and the power of enjoyment is bestowed by God. Building a relationship with Christ is like a rare and precious jewel. One treasures it more and more as one's love becomes deep and true.

God has symmetry on prosperity and adversity according to His law so that one is totally dependent upon God; and attains spiritual maturity (Ecclesiastes 7:14). Our God is faithful. The way to real gratitude is not to become more powerful or famous, but to become more human and tolerant. Seek God's direction in order to be wise and be intentional so you can grow in Christ.

Focusing on the Future

I recently attended a Christian concert with three of my sisters in Christ. The music was wonderful and spiritual. As I looked across the Celebrity Theater seating, it was clear that there were several youths who would have preferred to be somewhere else. However, the enjoyment of the concert was seen in the mother's face as she sang along. As I watched her I could only assume the mother's single-mindedness was on her children's future. I sensed that she was the one who deliberately chose the plan by which to guide her family in the right direction. Whether or not the kids enjoyed the concert or paid attention to the music was not the intent here. Her main objective was to provide the opportunity for the necessary seeds to be planted within her children and allow the Holy Spirit to work in their young lives.

When we forget what we have left behind and strive towards what is ahead, our sights are then focused on our future. By doing this, it allows us to press onward towards a possible future which God has called us to (Philippians 3:14). If we keep our sights on the past, we will miss out on what God's gifts, blessings and plans are for our lives. God created us on purpose, "He created my innermost being, you knit me together in my mother's womb," (Psalm 139:13) for a purpose. "For I know the plans I have for you" declares the Lord, plans to prosper you and not harm you, plans for a hope and a future," (Jeremiah 29:11). Knowing that God had a purpose for me was a good reason for seeking his face with all my heart. God has given me and you His promise that if we seek Him, we will be able to find Him (Psalm 119:58). God will make himself readily available to meet me whenever I call upon Him. Such assurances are not found in today's busy standards of living. If I do not carry a calendar in order to maintain an orderly sequence of schedules, I would be rushing to meet deadlines. That type of lifestyle is overly exerting and dangerous to one's health.

Have you ever noticed at times life simulates a race? Whether it be our job, education, or any aspect of our lives, moving in such a fast pace, we must continuously remember to remove, throw aside, or avoid everything that hinders and entangles us, so that we "May run with perseverance the race that is marked for us," (Hebrews 12:1). As I move towards the finish line, how can I achieve the purpose if my focus is removed from God? I cannot, if I do not hold onto the knowledge that God's words are true (John 16:13-15).

God does have a wonderful plan for our lives (Jeremiah 29:11), and that He has given us gifts which are within us to achieve his purpose (1 Corinthians 12:17). My surroundings trigger my emotions which allow me to perceive an event in a particular way, thereby arousing an emotional response. The problem arises from the thoughts which are produced by those emotions and the forthcoming behavior. Since emotions are spontaneous, they only last for a short period of time unless nurtured. Capturing the thought and replacing it with a positive behavior ensures growth.

Seasons come and seasons go and it is through those seasons our lives are formed. "See! The winter is past, the rains are over and gone. Flowers appear on earth; the season of singing has come" (Song of Songs 2:11-12). When I first decided to obey the Creator and commit my life to

Jesus Christ, I made a choice. The choice I made was to be crucified with Christ, to die from my old self and allow Christ to live in me (Galatians 2:20). Making such a significant life change was at first challenging and took a rigid daily regimen. Then as in any change, it became an integral and essential part of my daily living. I can no longer see my life without my Lord Jesus Christ leading the way. Without Him, the light currently radiating within my life would be bleak and oppressed and I would find myself living once again in a darkened dungeon. Therefore, I refuse to let go of the only thing in my life that gives me hope, joy, peace and an incredible future of an eternal life with God and His son Jesus Christ.

Focusing on the future whilst remembering that "If you believe, you will receive whatever you ask for in prayer," (Matthew 21:22); making everyday a joyful remembrance that although I will face hardships in my life, keeping the faith by knowing that I will finish the race and in the end I will receive the crown of righteousness (2 Timothy 4:7-8) is the ultimate gift that I want to receive from my Heavenly Father. There will be nothing greater than finishing the race and seeing the Lord Jesus Christ at the finish line, arms wide open and hearing Him say, I was a good and faithful servant. Availing ourselves to the gift of worshiping the Lord Jesus Christ, Wonderful Counselor, Mighty God, Everlasting Father, and Prince of Peace, (Isaiah 9:6) for all eternity.

Chapter Five

POWER OF GRATITUDE

Gratitude is an acknowledgement of God and who He is and what He has done. It is a heartfelt emotion independent of anyone else's response or upon any gift. Life is a gracious gift of God and should not be taken for granted. A spirit of gratitude should be cultivated with love towards the Creator, remembering always that a grateful person humbles himself when focusing on God. Enjoyment of life flows directly from gratitude for all that God provides (Ecclesiastes 8:15). God sustains the life of His creation (Psalm 23:1). His eternal unfailing purpose is to direct and guide His creation (Proverbs 3:6).

God expects from His children gratitude (1 Thessalonians 5:18). One should never take for granted the small and ordinary daily blessings (Matthew 6:11). Sometimes when we receive a blessing from God we forget to stop and say thank you to Him in whom all blessings abound. Gratitude leads us in the direction of and encourages us to draw closer to God. Our attitude changes and we see things in a different perspective, a positive one. Since we all have the ability to think, why not maintain an attitude of reverence and gratitude in the Supreme Being who continuously seek those who seek Him. Gratitude is the seed by which blessings are manifested. If my attitude is not one of gratitude, how then am I expected to get intimately acquainted with God? It would be inconceivable. It is only through our willingness to have a personal relationship with God that God will draw near to us (James 4:8).

Refusing to relinquish control of my life to God only brought out the fighter within me. Struggling to maintain control kept me from repentance. Working long hours to sustain myself as a Super Business Woman and a Super Single Mom stimulated my super-achievement ego daily. Then in a blink of an eye, the daily rush of adrenalin which invigorated and kept me energized was torn from my very essence. The change within the economic market rendered me another statistic. Angry and bitter I refused to admit to God that I was not and could not be sufficient in myself. Since my self-esteem, and sense of worth were eradicated the consideration of God's plan and priorities in my life were forbidden. I lost sight of the true importance while dealing with this devastating interruption. However, God's continuous loving support and faithfulness brought me back from the depths of despair.

Counting one's blessings in the mist of adversity and trials allows us to remember to thank God even during those times. Gratitude should always be shown to God, family and friends and should never be taking for granted. One should always look for blessings from God as well as recognize that not every gift you desire is beneficial to you.

An attitude of gratitude is a reflection of how I feel towards all the things, people, and circumstances surrounding my life. It is how I see my life unfolding as I realize I am no longer the captain of my life… Jesus Christ is. It was in this moment wherein I realized I could no longer live or breathe without my God and through the light of Christ which brought me out of darkness and into a future worth living.

Gratitude allows one to dream big dreams and reach for abundance not only for us but for our future generations. Acceptance of God's promises with reverent gratitude opens the doors for more gifts. Even when Jesus Christ prayed He held an attitude of gratitude towards His Father, always.

Gratitude is the attitude of thanksgiving in the midst of unwelcomed circumstances. Thanking God allows me to maintain a steadfast awareness of an affirmative state of increase. Counting my blessings daily makes me appreciate with wholehearted gratitude the God who loves me, the people in my life and the things I have accomplished. Gratitude also helps me to focus my inner thoughts on alleviating the constraints which prohibit me from appreciating the gifts in my life, and hinder my growth. Nothing has ever been achieved without gratitude and determination. It was only by the grace of God and the blood of Jesus Christ that I am here today. Thank you Lord!

Praise

My adulation is towards the God Almighty. It is adoration from the heart and the acceptance of the existence of a greater power than anyone can conceive on this earth. Praising is a form of worship, exalting, honoring, and glorifying God in the fullest measure possible. Praising God does not come easy to anyone especially since it is against our nature when in the midst of suffering. It can sometimes feel more like lip service than a true expression of one's feelings towards a loving God. Praise can be given whenever and wherever you are (Psalm 96:3).

Praising God during my feelings of worthlessness, dejection and hopelessness was totally alien and against my better judgment. Being under financial straits can alienate one from His grace and if you are like most of us, praising a loving God through times of extreme lows is the furthest thing from our minds. However, comprehending the significance behind the reason one should praise God during those unfortunate times empowers us with the best weapon against temptation and Satan. When we praise God, no matter what the circumstance – it shows the Heavenly Host, demons of darkness and all the spiritual realm that God is worthy of praise. Praise should genuinely come from the heart during times of sorrow, trials, discouragement, joy and peace. God delivers us, fulfills our desires and preserves us (Psalm 145:18-20), therefore isn't He worthy of praise?

At times even mature Christians can find praising God difficult while in the heart of adversity. Learning to change the way my thoughts perceived the circumstance in the middle of one of my lowest points, was not only challenging but demanded inner faith. There will be many occasions within our lives where we will feel as though God has turned away from us. Let me just say, no matter how difficult the situation may seem and how low my emotional state is, praising God during that period of adversity is the lifeline that keeps me strong. Praise also provides the means which maintains a set course to dissuade me from straying from the path prepared for me nor will it allow me to suffer complete defeat. Only with persistence did I learn to praise God in all things.

Praising God during our high moments is just a reminder of how we made it through the low seasons. "From the rising of the sun to the place where it sets, the name of the Lord is to be praised," (Psalm113:3). I have learned to never stop praising the God of heaven and earth for all that He has done and continues to do.

When I praise God, He responds with no less than an absolute abundance of unconditional love. My inner soul is enveloped in a feeling of pure joy and peace. It is a spiritual unconditional hug that can only be found in a personal relationship with Christ. One of the most valued treasures in any trial or suffering is the intimacy you will have with God. Praising God provides the opportunity necessary for God to work in my life, thus allowing myself to follow His plan through a blessed hope. How awesome it would be to hear the entire universe praising God! For that reason when I praise God no matter what my circumstances may be, praising produces victory, and when I am victorious it evokes praise.

You see, seeking God through praise provides the opportunity for God through his infinite knowledge and power to judge our hearts. Since God knows us better than we know ourselves, He understands our hearts, thoughts and our motivations. If I genuinely want to travel in the Lord's way and enjoy His presence, I must depend on God to lead me in the right way. He is the ultimate physician, the healer of all and worthy to be praised (Jeremiah 17:14). God is my rock and His word is perfect (Deuteronomy 32:3-4).

Thanksgiving

My youth, how incredibly distant it seems. Another life time in which God appeared to me, offering me a different future, yet, unbeknownst to me, I refused His invitation. I can only believe my refusal was owing to my overall ignorance of Scripture. Sixteen was undoubtedly a time of dreams and self-discovery. A self-fulfillment journey of youthful desires in which a declaration of loyalty to God was not proposed or intended to become a part of my plan; yet, throughout all the seasons of depression, loneliness, anguish and pain I, if only for a short time, ran to God for deliverance.

I am so thankful that God chose me as one of His children. He waited patiently for me to return from the life I was so determined to live out. A life centered on abuse and heartache. God is merciful and patient when it concerns His children as He is unwilling to allow any of his children to perish (Matthew 18:12-14). All anyone has to do is reach out and accept the gift of God's only Son, Jesus Christ as their Lord and Savior. I accepted His invitation and He welcomed me with open arms. He will do the same for you.

Sometimes thankful praise is our way of celebrating the Lord's righteous judgment. A thankful heart is an integral part of the holy life. Individuals who have a heart full of praise bring only joy to our Heavenly Host while glorifying His name. My spirit of thankfulness acknowledges who God truly is and His unfailing love in my life. Giving thanks in all circumstances while continuously praying especially through difficulties permits God's will to be reflected in us (1 Thessalonians 5:16-17).

However, most of society's attitude today is of thanklessness. Instead of being grateful for the blessings and gifts received from God, one tends to forget and become self-centered instead of Christ-centered. I have even complained that the gifts were not enough, while I went through great lengths to obtain more; even to the point of coveting and self-indulgence. Despite of that, I must remember if I am discontent with the Lord's judgments, provisions and plans, my faithlessness will bring great loss and pain. So why not replace anxious thoughts by simply freely offering thanksgiving from a heart established with trust in God as all sufficient? (Psalm 112:7-8; Philippians 4:6-7).

If one is to remain in God's grace, one should fight selfishness by offering heartfelt thanks to the Lord, and remembering that "He is the source of everything we have (Psalm 104) and the earth provides." I give thanks to my Lord every day since it was through Christ that I established my relationship with God, my Father. I am grateful for God establishing into law the rules and statues by which one should live. Devoid of set boundaries our lives would be chaotic. In following God's rules in my walk with Christ, God provided for the forgiveness of our sins (John 3:16-19), renewal of my life (2 Corinthians 5:16-21) and empowering me to carry out His works (Acts 1:6-8).

When I give thanks to the Lord, whether by praise or prayer, my expression of devotion to the Lord for saving me from my past and for trusting Him for my future deliverance, demonstrates the trust I have in God's promise.

Thinking Positively

Motivation and willingness is a requirement of changing ones thoughts and attitude. Popular psychology tells us that the way people think affects their emotions and attitude in the way they relate to others around them. It also affects the way one handles difficulties, trials and everyday stress. Psychology maintains that positive thinking increases one's contentment and one's accomplishments. In order for one to be motivated to maintain the positive thinking, in any given situation, whether it be weight loss, learning a new language, or just plain getting out of bed in the morning, one must understand that there is a higher power source which provides for our every need, even if one does not believe or accept it.

There is a figure of speech that we are all accustomed to which says "You are what you eat." Therefore one has to acknowledge the fact that whatsoever is spoken from ones mouth derives directly from the heart (Matthew 12:34). In order to become an advancing person, transformation has to take place. No longer would I conform to my old desires in my patterns of thinking and behaving (1 Peter 1:13-16). The way I think will naturally affect my actions, which consequently will dictate the end results. Altering our thought process and maintaining positive thinking will result in increased happiness and success in life.

Every rung of the ladder contains obstacles in the road to achieving success. Those obstacles produce negative thought patterns. Becoming aware of my surroundings and how those surroundings influenced my thinking provided the necessary strength and ability to potentially change my end results. My last encounter with my former employer gave rise to thoughts of depression, subjugation and triviality.   Capturing those negative thoughts through the aid of the Holy Spirit, although extremely challenging at first, allowed for the proliferation of affirmative ones. "Lord...help me! Hear my prayer and keep me from deceitful ways," I prayed. His insults and mockery were beyond the ability of any normal person's emotional threshold. Yet, enduring his insolent nature gave rise to a spiritual discernment and a passionate vision.

Thinking positively during circumstances which denotes otherwise is extremely difficult, but one which can be achieved. If we make God's thoughts our thoughts, we are then able to begin the process of thinking positively. This can only be achieved through Him, who provides strength and can do everything (Philippians 4:13). However, this trait can only be achieved not just through our personal effort but rather through the assistance of the Holy Spirit. At times situations arose wherein I had no other option than to persistently ask the Holy Spirit to indwell in me, in facilitating my growth while I preserved a positive mental outlook. As Christians we are called to be positive thinkers (Philippians 4:11). In order to achieve this mental ability, we must accept and believe God's will in our lives. Subsequently, the result will be one of habitually conforming our thinking and behavior to God's Word over a lifetime.

Evolution of one's inner being is through meditation on all things which are true, noble, just, pure, lovely and of good report (Philippians 4:8). Our thoughts should be virtuous and praiseworthy. Thinking anything other than positive thoughts will cause one to falter in one's development. For without it, we find that we are powerless to fight the evil in our minds. The condition of our hearts ultimately determines the condition of our thoughts (Matthew 15:19). When we allow our mind to dwell on negative and destructive thoughts the vibrations associated with those thoughts will eventually trigger and cause to produce that which we permit our minds to occupy, manifesting themselves into ungodly thoughts and speech (Jude 15:10).

One motivation should be to impress upon oneself the desire for positive thinking to please the spirit with the end result of reaping a harvest of plentitude (Galatians 6:9). Positive thinking is an avenue which allows me to embrace the good news of Jesus Christ, while enthusiastically celebrating the Lord's faithfulness, His committed mercy, forgiveness and unfailing love, by sending His only begotten son to fulfill the plan for which it was intended (John 3:16), my salvation. An individual who truly wants to advance in life does so with mental dedication towards achieving the overall goal of increase.

God's Mercy

My lifestyle has placed demands upon me which necessitate long hours of dedication. At times, my professional dedication breached my personal relationship with the Almighty. When this occurs, it produces a sense of unworthiness, leaving within me the impression that God's mercy is unobtainable. I have arrived at the understanding that when I feel God's mercy completely gone, it is because I have intentionally placed an impediment between myself and my Lord Jesus Christ. Then it is I who has to draw closer to God, when my daily haste keeps me separated from Him. God is always there waiting faithfully and patiently. He understands that our lives are exceptionally busy with family, friends, work and hobbies. God wants to be a part of our "ENTIRE" life, not just a "PART" of it.

At times, being unattached produces feelings of loneliness. When that occurs remembering to distinguish between God's presence and the feeling of the fact, produces a feeling of camaraderie with the Lord. During those instances my soul feels lonely and deserted I speak a few words of faith – "Lord even though I do not see you or feel your presence, I know you are mercifully here." At other times when I am unsure of why there is no connection and I feel a vast expanse of space between us, I can be assured of the promise that God's mercy is great (1 Kings 3:6), abundant (1 Peter 1:3), and everlasting (Psalm 103:17).

Working under such tyrannical conditions does not leave room for a system of mercy; especially those whose social status does not require them to scale the ladder of success. Working until midnight and weekends to beat the deadlines went unnoticed and unappreciated. Yet, coming to the realization that my life was one sided left my life unbalanced and unfulfilled. Existence without my God throws my life into disarray. Life becomes distorted and unrewarding, upsetting the very nature of my being. Being under the umbrella of God's mercy produces a sense of wellbeing for it is God's gift to those who place their faith in Christ.

We are a sinful generation, yet God's mercy is compassion in action towards those who sin and have no right to receive such treatment. Making the Lord the source of our supply generates delight in knowing His mercy is made new with every sunrise. To those who are anxious and willing to keep God's promises of faithfulness and love during punishment will endure forever.

Since God is a merciful God He loves both you and I. He shows everlasting kindness and mercy on all His children (Isaiah 54:8). Our Heavenly Father shows His love like a mother shows compassion towards her child. As a result when we stray, the Lord disciplines those He loves and punishes each one He accepts as His child (Hebrews 12). When I have intentionally placed an impediment between myself and my Lord Jesus Christ, my awareness becomes keen to the pressures and anxieties I personally placed upon myself. Thus disciplinary action is to be expected. Being disciplined according to my disobedience only reflects and proves God's merciful love.

One thing is for sure God does not treat us the way we deserve to be treated, nor does He treat us with disrespect. God's mercy is depicted in geographical proportions as vast as the expanse which separates the heavens from the earth and as far as the east is from the west (Psalm 103:12). God is righteous therefore He is just to those who are oppressed. He loves us so passionately that He is "Merciful and gracious, slow to anger, and abounding in mercy," (Psalm 103:8) and to those who believe, He is the source of our mercies, and mercy will never fail us.

Worship

Ah…now we have come to my favorite chapter - worship. We are so blessed to be able to freely worship our God without fear of repercussion from our government. There are so many countries where this freedom does not exist or death is the measurement of punishment dispensed. Worship is a privilege to a God who has dominion over all the earth and all who dwell in it (Psalm 24:3-5).

As I write this, my thoughts flow back to a time when I had a particular conversation with God. I was still a young Christian and yearned desperately to worship God wholeheartedly. My deepest desire was to attain the freedom to openly raise my arms while singing in worship, announcing to the world that yes…I adored my God for giving me the freedom from the bonds that oppressed me. One morning as I was getting ready for Church, I was in the middle of blow drying my hair when I began a conversation with God "Lord," I said. "I want to raise my hands to you while worshipping, but I am afraid. My fear is so intense, it overtakes me. Lord, when my spirit urges me to lift my arms to the heavens, my mind takes me to the edge of a vast precipice. I begin to sweat and my heart begins to pound. No!" I hear a voice saying in my mind. "Don't raise your hands Jenny, people will stare!" Many foolish and ill-advised thoughts were running through my mind denying the impulse of my spirit. "Father, my spirit is willing but my flesh is weak. Help me Lord to break free and move past the fear barrier and I ask this in the name of your son Jesus Christ." Amen. I thanked God as I hurried out of the house.

I have to stop here a moment and say God does in fact listen. "His eyes move to and fro seeking those who are loyal and devoted to the Him (2 Chronicles 16:9) and when you ask for God's involvement to ensure your growth in His word, God will use whatever method at His disposal to respond and reveal His purpose for you. It may be through the radio or television media, a family member, a friend, via the internet or just a complete stranger. You will never know in what form God will respond, however, if you remember to be still and listen (Psalm 46:10) God will reply.

I arrived at church and sat down at my usually location, first row center. It had a great view of the band. The service started and I began to sing loudly. Mentally preparing myself for worship, I moved as close to the edge of the precipice as I dared by raising my arms to my waist. "Not bad," I told myself. The service concluded. I was standing talking to some friends when I noticed the drummer heading in my direction from the stage. "Hi Artie," I said. "How are you doing?" Artie stared at me and said "You know…you can raise your arms higher" and walked away. He left me dumbfounded! God sent someone I knew to reassure and convey the message "I heard you my child and we will work on it together." From that moment on my fears diminished. With each service my arms reached higher and higher towards the heavens. I did it! I broke through the fear barrier!

My heart now overflows with joy when I enter into my time of worship. My spirit rejoices as worshipping allows me to go before my Lord in reverence and awe. Yet, before I can truly go before the Lord, I must first be of a pure and sincere heart, thus allowing a more intimate relationship with God. It is an experience like none other. Nothing in this world could ever compare with such joy of fellowship with the Creator. When I go before the Lord in worship it glorifies God. Worshipping requires inner purity towards our Maker (John 4:24).

When I worship it provides the avenue by which I can freely reveal my appreciation, sincerity, honesty and integrity to God. Freely worshiping the Lord is a great honor and is essential in building my relationship with Him. When I first decided to turn my life over to God, I did not know nor could I ever imagine such a demonstrative and freeing sense of emotional existence! Worshipping is the very essence of what it means to be a believer. It is spontaneous praise and prayer and should be integrated in everyday life while rendering worship to God only. Every beautiful moment should be spent enjoying the closeness one achieves during the act of worship.

It is through Christ that we can come before God with freedom and without fear. We can do this through faith in Christ (Ephesians 3:12). God grants me the desire to always look to Christ for guidance, to walk with Him in times of adversities, to hold steadfast to His promises, to believe in His unwavering faith when the burden of crushing weight in upon me; and even when a stinging blow falls on my life. Lord, help me to remember that no matter the circumstance, I am to worship you, honor you and wait patiently for you to help me and restore me.

Chapter Six

REWARDS

I previously stated how our thoughts and actions determine the outcome and the direction of our lives. The decision I made in my teens in chasing my own ideals as an alternative to owing up to God's calling, spiraled me into a future of unhappiness drenched in a roller coaster of painful abuse. Unable to accept responsibility for my decisions only paved a highway of regret, culpability and reproach towards God. Many times I found myself focusing on work rather than dealing with the circumstance at hand; laboring continuously without just rewards. I assumed that if I worked long hours I would eventually catch up with time or even conquer it. That of course, was an erroneous assessment. Nevertheless, my insatiable desire to acquire possessions by squandering my hard earn money was the means by which I chose to reward myself when faced with life's disappointments.

Nonetheless, we are so conditioned to go through life with only one focus - ourselves. Self-indulgence only takes away our focus from our Lord Jesus Christ. Consequently, is it not logical to presume that inappropriate actions would not call for discipline? Since discipline would be its just punishment. Thus accomplishments and excelling also dictate just rewards. Assuredly, it is common sense. Deciding to accept Jesus

Christ as my Lord and Savior produced in me an unimpaired attitude and restored my physical health where God had initially planned for me; and in so doing opened avenues for future blessings by my willingness to continue focusing on God's word and His perfect law which also grants me the freedom I desire (James 1:25). Being in God's will, while standing firm allow our prayers to be answered and our deliverance to be obtained (Exodus 14:13).

God's desire is for all His children to receive the gift of salvation, blessings and prosperity. "God will give us the desires of our heart," (Mark 11:24) if we devote ourselves to prayer while thanking God for all we have been given (Colossians 4:12). We should never be afraid to go before the Lord in prayer for things we desire. For nothing is too big or too small for God. However, do not make the mistake of assuming that your blessings will be forthcoming if your motives are for selfish indulgence (James 4:2-3). Spending time with the Lord daily pleases God. Again, prayers are answered if they are asked for in God's will. If we learn to be patient and wait on Him, the blessings would be more incredible than we could ever imagine. For when we do, God's blessings are immeasurable.

Inheritance

The majority of the population is hard working with a vocation or occupation. Their lifelong dream is to work laboriously in an attempt to achieve the final goal of riches and retirement. I am one of those who have labored for many years in hopes of bestowing upon my son an inheritance upon my departure from this life (Proverbs 13:22). It is a parent's desire to prevent, if at all possible, their children's suffering by providing them with the opportunity to advance further than their parents own accomplishments. If that goal is achievable, then the end results can be attained for future generations.

There is, however, a simpler way of attaining an everlasting inheritance. The inheritance which I have just mentioned can easily be accomplished through the acceptance of Jesus Christ as one's Lord. This acknowledgment and acceptance of Jesus Christ opens up doors into the Kingdom as a gift to you from your Creator. Once a decision is made to accept Christ as your Lord and Savior, it is then that you become a child of God with the full measure and rights bestowed upon all God's children, and who are blessed with the knowledge that we are heirs, and co-heirs with Christ Jesus (Romans 8:17).

It was through my faith in God's son Jesus Christ which justifies me, as a believer, gave me hope and gained entrance into my future inheritance. Given that we are now the children of God, one can rest assure that the promise and down payment of the Holy Spirit awaits those who follow, and believe in Christ Jesus. It is the promise of being with our Lord Jesus Christ for all eternity.

It was through the great power of God's love which predestined us to be heirs as adopted sons and daughters through our Lord Jesus Christ (Ephesians 1:4-5). The great inheritance is being prepared for us in heaven (John 14:1-3). It was God's intended plan and purpose to bring everything together for good and only through God's grace do we belong to the Father, as His heirs. The book of Matthew provides a glimpse of God's attributes, in that if I as a single parent can lovingly and willingly provide everything for the care and welfare of my own son, how then can I not believe that the Creator of all things provide immeasurably more (Matthew 7:10)? It is so wonderful to know that as His children we are lavished with His love (James 3:1). He has redeemed us and adopted us. So when God starts His good works in us, we have God's assurance that He will not slow down nor stop working until it is carried out and finished on the day of Christ Jesus (Philippians 1:3-6).

I am not saying that once we accept Jesus Christ our lives will no longer have worries, trials or unhappiness. On the contrary, we will be able to walk in the knowledge that we are no longer confined to a life of solitude but to a life of solidarity with God. This harmonious relationship will provide the reinforced strength necessary to hold onto during our most vulnerable weaknesses.

Maintaining a steadfast attitude protects me from attaining lazy tendencies while teaching me the necessary aptitudes to imitate those who through faith and patience inherit what has been promised (Hebrews 6:2). Let me propose this…why not wait on the Lord? You truly have nothing to lose, yet everything to gain. Eternity is closer than you think.

God's Promises

Everyone has had promises broken at one time or another. Either by family, friends, co-worker, or even a special someone who may have intentionally or unintentionally broken their promises, which left us hurt, lost, emotionally wounded, or even in financial straits. We have come to accept a broken heart as a part of life, yet we somehow manage to get ourselves back on our feet.

However, after several broken promises, one begins to build a wall, one brick at a time. As promises are broken or one becomes hurt, a new brick is purposely cemented into position upon the wall until finally the wall is completed and one becomes less caring and hardened by life itself. That is exactly what my life had become. My emotions were safe behind the wall of impenetrability, a haven from the world of falsehoods and lies. I embraced the wall which rightly became my powerful protector operating as my emotional shield.

Upon reflection, although the walls protected me from my abusers reaching me emotionally, it also preserved the hurt and anger within the same compound. Only fueling the fire of increased abhorrence I felt towards those who hurt me. Hate began controlling my life, leaving me with a sense of misery and ill will. However, a ray of light shined as a beacon of hope through my dark and dismal surroundings. That beacon was my saving grace, my son Daniel.

Jesus avails Himself and utilizes whatever means for His loving purpose. Unbeknownst to me He employed my son. The love for my son was the means used in directing me to look deep within my inner most being and allow the healing process to begin. Trying to deliberately work through all those hateful issues and related ideas such as guilt, worthlessness, insignificant persona and zero self-esteem, I became aware of just how Jesus Christ was working in me. I was grateful for His faithfulness.

During the course of my studies, it became more evident that God made promises to His children and kept them. You and I can rest assured and depend on God fulfilling His promise always. Some of the promises are: how, we, His children who love Jesus Christ inherit the kingdom (James 2:5); how God promises comfort to all who ask (Isaiah 12:1); when we are deserted by family and friends. God welcomes us (Psalm 7:10); how the poor are delivered from trouble (Psalm 34:6); and when we are tempted, God will provide a way out (1 Corinthians 10:13).

I found numerous more promises throughout the Scriptures. Those were only just a few. The list is never ending. His unfailing, unconditional love is God's greatest promise to us. Walking through a life of broken promises, it is comforting to know that He shall never leave us nor forsake us (Hebrews 13:5). What a wonderful promise! It is a promise no one can ever break; for this promise is not made by man but by God once we accept God's son Jesus Christ. His promises are that of abundant blessings. It is only through the blood of Jesus Christ that we are saved!

Acceptance

All our lives we strive for acceptance from our parents, family, friends, teachers, and co-workers. Yet, the more one moves towards achieving that goal, the more it becomes elusive. How hard does one have to strive to gain acceptance by those who one respects? It becomes harder if our sins are made known and one received public discipline. The cost for acceptance now reaches even higher stakes. Society has a different take on how sinfulness is viewed. Acceptance can be difficult to obtain when one performs outside the social norms. So, how does one achieve acceptance if all one has ever known is rejection? I learned firsthand the plight one had to endure in hopes of one day achieving acceptance in my former marriage.

Although I loved and accepted by husband with all his faults, he was incapable of distinguishing between a love from a mother and the love of a wife. An innocent child seeking through childhood and into adulthood acceptance and approval; yet, never achieving acceptance from his mother only led to a life filled with deep regret, egoism, self-absorption, and an arrogant lifestyle. Confronted with feelings of rejection and the comparison to other men, he felt inadequate, insecure, frustrated, and helpless as he faced the challenges of life. During those times I endeavored through loving words and actions to accept him, the more he refused my love, striving ultimately to acquire it from his mother. Those were difficult years in our marriage.

One night, many years later after our separation, I received a call from Paul. I was shocked! My number was unlisted. How did he manage to acquire my number? He apologized for all the years of heartache. His lack of awareness in God's purpose for a husband and wife was proven throughout our marriage. Genesis 2:24 illustrates how a man once married, is to leave his father and mother and become one with his wife, thus making it possible for him to acquire and receive the acceptance from his significant other…his wife.

On the road of life one will always meet with failure. My failure was striving to meet unreasonable demands placed upon me by an individual whose acceptance no matter what I accomplished or the commitment and dedication afforded, would never be forthcoming.

The wonderful truth is that we can rely on the knowledge that we can maintain a blessed hope of the existence of a God who will accept us even if no one else does. No matter what we have done, it is through the words of Peter that we are reassured "That God does not show favoritism but accepts men from every nation who fear him and do what is right," (Acts 10:34-35). It is God's gift to His children. God accepts us for whom and what we are, even if we fall short of society's measure.

Blessings

My life has been filled with much sorrow, trials, financial chaos, oppression, threats, physical & mental abuse, and failed marriages. In spite of that, I have come to realize that God was present in my life. For each season facilitated and increased my character development. For great character is not developed through luxurious living, but is achieved through suffering.

To be acquainted with and become familiar with God is the greatest blessing any human being can discern and experience. If we learn to walk in a positive and contented state, our attitude will equip and drive us in a direction to receive other blessings (Psalm 1:1-3). The blessing that I received from Jesus Christ was an epiphany when I finally became aware of how much God's desire was to continuously bless me and "Give me the desires of my heart," (Psalm 37:4).

Blessings and rich rewards are all part of God's plan for our lives. Total obedience is the shortest route between us and the life we desire, but only if we trust God completely and are willing to obey Him completely. With that in mind, we should always seek out and do everything according to His will. Remember when I chose to do it my way? When I arrived at my first crossroad of life, did I answer God's call? No…I chose the path of destruction, which led me to a life of beatings, abuse, drug, lies and adultery. Recognizing that I no longer wanted to operate out of a position of fear, lack and limitation, as I had previously been conditioned to, I, through faith instinctly became aware that I had the power to change my life!

After twenty years of my life being submerged in darkness, sadness, financial stress, abuse, pain and heartache, I desperately wanted to become one of God's children. Directing all my energies towards God's light. I frantically began to swim towards the direction of the light, learning to become steadfast in my prayers as prayers linked me with the Sovereign God in a phenomenal way. I failed in my own life; I was not intending to fail in prayer as a new child of God (1 Samuel 12:23).

Although I have suffered for many years, my life has been thoroughly blessed. The blessings were all encompassing as I have received the gift of a wonderful son, family and great friends, but the unsurpassed reward is the love of my Heavenly Father bestowed upon me through the incredible gift of his Son, Jesus Christ.

Prayer places me in a harmonious state to go before the Lord. It humbles me and puts me right with God. I know that I am able to go confidently before God in prayer and when I pray in the will of God, I understand and accept that I have already received that which I asked for. It is the drive behind His blessings and the reason for His compassion, kindness, and generosity (Psalm 84:11). God does not give out of obligation, for He is never in anyone's debt. He gives out of His goodness.

If you truly desire an abundant life, it can truly be achieved through the power of prayer. We sometimes pray for things we do not need or even pray for things we need but do not want. We should never pray selfish prayers. God's blessings are abundantly bestowed upon all who love and follow Him. The blessings from God are not merely a reward for just being good, but a gift given to us by our Heavenly Father. Although blessings are given to each of His children in different measures, one should always remember that no matter how small or how big the blessings are, they are still being sent down to us by God and thereby God should always be remembered with thanksgiving. Blessings are the outcome of obedience and for the purpose of glorifying God.

Prosperity

Self sacrifice will make you a success in business. Those around you will commend you if you are prosperous, yet one should remember that "Every good and perfect gift is from above, coming down from the Father of the heavenly lights," (James 1:17). I am extremely grateful and thankful to God for giving me the opportunity to consider my ways, granting me strength and determination to change my life by refocusing my priorities and my desire to become a better person in Christ.

I made a decision for myself and my family to serve the Lord (Joshua 24:15) and continue in His will. Because God is such a loving, compassionate and discipline Lord who continues to save me from myself. I am unable to start my day without first entrusting it to the Lord's care (Proverbs 16:3) otherwise my daily goals would be unreachable. God is an Omnipotent Being; he is around us all the time. God is an Omnipresent Being; he is everywhere at once. He is also an Omnipotent Being; an all powerful God.

Let me take a moment to reiterate - God has a plan and purpose for our lives. If one is to prosper, one must first connect one's desire; one's will and make one's plans…God's plans. I learned to change my conditioning and renew my mind about my current reality to one of acceptance through faith. If my thoughts continued to be physical, then my desires and financial income would have remained immoral, self-indulgent, depraved and spent on sinning (Romans 6:23). God is a good God and can not dwell in sin.

However, prosperity can be bestowed if one continues to seek God's wisdom in both the spiritual and natural intellect while applying ourselves attentively to the work God has appointed us to do. I pray every day that God would grant me and allow the Holy Spirit to guide me in every aspect of my life, while obeying and loving God. Do this and "God will make you most prosperous in all the works of your hands," (Deuteronomy 30: 9-10).

I have learned the hard way to follow in the manner and the direction the Lord determined for my life. My life has never been the same since that night in May. Jesus Christ, the Son of the Living God. He has NEVER failed me nor will He ever fail me. He has NEVER broken a promise to me. If you will seek God's wisdom and through a devoted commitment live a righteous life according to God's teachings, then God will cause material prosperity to come upon you and "All these things will be added unto us," (Matthew 6:33). For when I am faithful to God's ways, He freely bestows prosperity upon me (Psalm 128:1-2). God is not against material wealth, if the wealth and prosperity is used to do "Good works, ready to give, willing to share," (1 Timothy 6:17-19).

God is ready to entrust us with all the necessary resources for our lives and for His future ministry through us. Always remember to give thanks in all circumstances. Those whose minds are sufficiently renewed in God's will and commands are destined for *JUST* Rewards.

Your Invitation to have a
Personal Relationship with Jesus Christ

For all of us who have suffered, been left alone to provide for your own children, have been through divorce, physical or mental abuse, financial straits, health problems, family and relational problems, abandonment, incarceration or just have questions that need answers, I'd like to take this opportunity to introduce you to a God who in his compassion showed us how much He loved us by sending his only precious Son Jesus Christ to die on the cross for us (John 3:16). As a final sacrificial Lamb for the salvation of all who seek Him, believe in Him and accept Jesus Christ as their Lord and Savior. "God has freed us from the power of darkness and He brought us into the kingdom of His dear Son," (Colossians 1:13). Christ himself paid a hefty price for us. It was through Christ own body on the cross which unites us all as one, by breaking down the wall of hostility. For through Christ, we can now come before the Father through the same Holy Spirit.

If you are ready to accept Jesus Christ into your heart and experience a life of unfailing love, then just say this heartfelt prayer to yourself...

Father, I humbly come before you to ask you to forgive me of my sins. I know Father that I am unworthy for I have lived a sinful life. I accept your Son Jesus Christ as my Lord and Savior who so willingly gave himself in my stead as the last sacrificial Lamb. Cleanse me Father from my past life and help me to learn to walk in your righteous ways.

Thank you Father, in the name of Jesus Christ I pray. Amen!

JESUS LOVES YOU!

JUST Rewards

To order additional copies of *JUST* **Rewards,** complete the following:

Ship to: (please print)

Name _____

Address _____

City _____, State _____, Zip _____

Phone # _____

_____ copies of *JUST* **Rewards**

@ $12.99 each $ _____

Shipping and handling @ $3.50 per book $ _____

Total amount enclosed $_____

Please make checks payable to: Pastor Jenny Fisher
 And Send to: P.O. Box 1993, El Mirage, Arizona 85335

You may e-mail the author at: jennyfisherministries@hotmail.com

www.ingramcontent.com/pod-product-compliance
Lightning Source LLC
LaVergne TN
LVHW021350080426
835508LV00020B/2199